PEACEFUL PARENTING

BY THE SAME AUTHOR

The Gamer's Inheritance

Coom, Consume, Comply

Torturing The Villagers

Make Self-Knowledge Great Again

Peaceful Parenting

Steven Franssen

Contents

Chapter One: Introduction

The public schooling systems across the West have failed to educate children in the most essential areas of knowledge for the continuance of civilization. As a result, public discourse continues to plummet, more and more people believe they are entitled to take what they want when they want, and civil conflict is erupting in all corners of our society. At the time of this writing, the economic and political ravages of COVID-19 continue to put pressure on parents who rely on the public schools in order to bring in two incomes for their families and somehow stay afloat. The US Centers for Disease Control and Prevention (CDC) has issued[1] draconian school reopening guidelines as such:

- Strict social distancing tactics

- All-day mask wearing for most students and teachers

- Staggered attendance

- Daily health checks

- No gym or cafeteria use

---

[1] https://www.zerohedge.com/political/back-school-no-thanks-say-millions-newly-homeschooling-parents

- Restricted playground access and limited toy-sharing, and

- Tight controls on visitors to school buildings, including parents.

The government encroachment into the family has become intolerable for most longtime Americans. Teachers are retiring en masse and nearly a third of parents say they are "very likely" to purse at-home learning options rather than send their kids in to the schools[2]. Millions of parents are turning away from government solutions to their personal challenges and homeschooling continues to come of age, continuing a strong trend that originally took root after George W. Bush's disastrous No Child Left Behind legislation.

With the increased need for at-home solutions for education, so increases the need for parenting solutions that make sense and *work*. Women are beginning to stay home again, writes The Wall Street Journal, "A survey conducted this spring by the Boston Consulting Group found that, on average, women were spending 15 hours more a week on domestic labor than men were, at 65 hours versus 50 hours, compared with a pre-Covid balance of 35 hours and 25 hours.[3]" Family time is going up and divorce rates are skyrocketing, particularly among newlyweds.[4] People, it seems, have forgotten how relationships work – absent the rampant careerism and consumerism of the last two generations. We can no longer avoid one another with coffee benders and long hours at the desk. We cannot whittle away the weekends with mass entertainment because production values have plunged and there is nothing all that fresh

---

2

https://www.usatoday.com/story/news/education/2020/05/26/coronavirus-schools-teachers-poll-ipsos-parents-fall-online/5254729002/

[3] https://www.wsj.com/articles/womens-careers-could-take-long-term-hit-from-coronavirus-pandemic-11594814403

[4] https://nypost.com/2020/09/01/divorce-rates-skyrocket-in-u-s-amid-covid-19/

or interesting going on in the way of culture with social media. Pew Research has found:

> The coronavirus outbreak has pushed millions of Americans, especially young adults, to move in with family members. The share of 18- to 29-year-olds living with their parents has become a majority since U.S. coronavirus cases began spreading early this year, surpassing the previous peak during the Great Depression era.[5]

All the usual distractions are being stripped away by the coming age of austerity. The bill is due for all the free stuff that was given away, both in the First World and as an ultra-massive and quickly squandered wealth transfer to the Third World. We are huddling together. The easiest victims in this stressful scenario are the children. They are little. They are vulnerable. They are weak. They require care and attention. Yet, we have found ourselves in this mess precisely because the Baby Boomers and Gen X'ers were plopped in front of TVs and liberal professors until their brains rotted. We are in this mess because Millennials were sent to expensive, low quality daycare and then indebted to Marxist professors, with porn as the weekend getaway between plummeting-wage service industry shifts. Things are a mess! People are less and less convinced they want to participate in the vicious cycle that has brought our empire to ruin. Everyone is looking for a new way.

This book posits peaceful parenting as the new way. With peaceful parenting, young parents will:

-spare their children the intergenerational conflict and addiction that has put us in this societal predicament

---

[5] https://www.pewresearch.org/fact-tank/2020/09/04/a-majority-of-young-adults-in-the-u-s-live-with-their-parents-for-the-first-time-since-the-great-depression/

-keep their children free and clear of the socialist indoctrination camps the public schools have become

-help build trust in the family that has been lost to a toxic culture helmed by a hostile elite

-empower themselves to better understand how children learn

-engender a culture of love, fun, order, and joy within the home

Parenting well leads to improved outcomes. We are entering an age where every advantage proffered will compound in a way heretofore unseen. Children who are parented well *today* will see themselves take up the tribal, civic, and economic mantles of the future. Parents of today who parent peacefully will age gracefully and in the care of loved ones.

I am a peaceful parent and Master of Arts in Teaching educator with a five-year career in direct education and approaching a decade of work as a consultant helping parents and aspiring parents to improve the moral and philosophical conditions of their lives. It is a great privilege for me to speak to you on the subject of parenting in this book. Together we can build a better future for our people and undo the havoc that has accrued across the globe. It is our moral imperative as reasoning people to bring the light of reason to our most personal relationships. Together we can stave off the darkness of barbarism and horrific child abuse threatening to snuff out forever the advantages our forefathers struggled and died to carve out for us these past two millennia. Before we get far into what peaceful parenting *is*, let us dive into what peaceful parenting *is not*.

Chapter Two: First Principles

In order to build the case for peaceful parenting, first we have to lay down the basics. What *is* peaceful parenting?

Peaceful parenting is the commitment to reasoning with children through all stages of their development. It is the methodology for raising children free of trauma and with full respect to the child's personhood, livelihood, and moral development

Trauma is the psychological, mental, and physical effects of child abuse. Trauma is most commonly expressed through the neurosis and psychosis that result from repressed feelings that are a reaction to trauma. We know this as addiction.

Addiction

We live in an addicted society. Look all around you. Everywhere you see people who are slaves to their impulses. The adult obesity rate in the United States is 42.4%.[6] Obesity is commonly an adult reaction to sexual molestation or objectification in childhood. People shroud themselves in body fat to turn away the sexual advances of others. Another precursor to obesity is a general feeling of emptiness in the home. There is not enough

---

[6] https://www.cdc.gov/obesity/data/adult.html

love…but there is food. Food is permitted. Sedate lifestyles are permitted. People fill themselves with food to gain temporary mastery over the hole in their hearts. All addictions are temporary reprieves from psychic pain from trauma experienced in childhood. Notice the vast numbers of people everywhere you go who are addicted to their devices. Their social lives were empty growing up. There are far fewer extended families intact compared to a couple generations ago. Nobody has cousins. People move away from their home states, pursuing their careers. Mothers have moved out of the home as taxation rates have gone up and "women's rights" are "championed" by hostile elites. People, classically termed "narcissists", are desperate for attention. They are chronically lonely. They turn to their devices for temporary dopamine bumps that have been masterfully orchestrated by Big Tech via the notification bell.

Look at the opioid epidemic. From 1998 to 2018, overdose deaths from prescription painkillers skyrocketed. Beginning in 2013, the death rate significantly increased due to the importation of illicitly manufactured Chinese fentanyl, a highly toxic synthetic opioid.[7] Americans are in pain. Indeed, it is painful to live in today's America. Americans have been legally dispossessed, deracinated by the mass media and government, shackled by stagnant wages, flooded by foreigners with hostile cultures, robbed of earning potential and currency value by bankers and politicians, and degraded by critical race theory peddled by open Marxists with considerable institutional power. There is no self-discovery left in American culture for the average American. The 1800's saw a strong middle class of people who were self-reflective and spread out evenly through the rural and suburban areas as landlords, yeoman gentry, and owners of manufacturing. The America of today is vastly different, with the economy pumped up like a cocaine addict through the issuance of debt by the banks and a horrible housing crunch where there

---

[7] https://www.cdc.gov/drugoverdose/epidemic/index.html

is a race to the bottom since no one owns anything anymore. Middle America was sold on lies and then laughed at by everyone else while the drugs poured in to serve as the societal coping mechanism.

Aside from substances and obesity, we can look at the epidemic of depression yet again cresting to new heights in the wake of the coronavirus social engineering, "Americans are reporting symptoms of depression three times more than they were before the pandemic, according to a recent study published in JAMA."[8] People are not allowed to see one another smile. They are made to wear masks. People must stay apart from one another, as they have to "socially distance". This is the dead inner life of government and corporate, Big Pharma bureaucrats being sprung upon the rest of society as a coordinated attack, for the rise of populism in the West has provoked intolerable feelings in these, for lack of a better term, lizard people. Everywhere we look across America there is a psychic attack well underway on the working families who make up the bedrock of our virtuous order. Many, many people are succumbing.

Peaceful parenting offers relief from the storm of collective psychosis and addiction. By helping yourself out of your addictions, you grant your children your hard-earned knowledge of recovery so that they may live to aspire to a better example. The Bill Gates', Anthony Fauci's, Joe Biden's, and Oprah Winfrey's of the world were raised to provoke addiction in others and to use verbal manipulation to achieve their ambitions. These people are leading the attack on American families all while working to convince families that they have the panacea for the ills that spread across the land. Peaceful parenting makes children addiction-

---

[8] https://www.axios.com/mental-health-coronavirus-pandemic-depression-suicide-c09ad125-10a9-44b0-a91d-ca40656816aa.html

resistant and thus less likely to fall prey to these kinds of manipulators.
From American Addiction Centers:

> Children of parents with substance abuse issues are at greater
> risk for abuse or neglect, and this childhood abuse will have a
> devastating impact throughout their lives. These children are
> more likely to experience trauma, face difficulties with
> concentration and learning, control their physical and emotional
> responses to stress, and form trusting relationships. Several
> epidemiological studies have shown that experiencing abuse as a
> child increases the risk for substance abuse later in life. Adults
> who were abused as children often turn to drugs and alcohol as a
> coping mechanism for dealing with their childhood trauma.
> Results from a long-term study following abused children up to
> the age of 24 showed that physical abuse during the first five
> years of life predicts subsequent substance use later in life.[9]

The link between childhood trauma and addiction in adulthood is a hard
and fast fact. Addicts raise addicts. The economy, culture, government,
and politics are all juiced up with addiction. We live in an age of powerful
predators and a few shepherds who still have the power to hold back total
anarchy. Peaceful parenting builds up new shepherds to guard the flock
against these power-hungry abusers. Remove abuse from the home and
you begin to remove abuse from the broader community.

Self-Ownership

A critical, early first principle to mention on behalf of peaceful parenting
is the idea of self-ownership. As adults, we own our bodies. Slavery is
immoral. Hundreds of thousands of Americans died to establish this as
incontrovertible fact. Now, hostile foreigners who engage in sex-

---

[9] https://americanaddictioncenters.org/blog/the-link-between-child-
abuse-and-substance-abuse

trafficking, human-trafficking, child-trafficking, and open-air market slave auctions are coming to America and trying to get us all to forget this fundamental fact.

Since we own our bodies, we are responsible for the safekeeping of our bodies. Our bodies are temples, sacred and to be taken care of so that we may do good works and effect virtue in the world. Property rights flow from self-ownership. We mix our labor with materials, land, and tools and engage in trade and enterprise with others. The more robust and respected our property rights in a given society, the wealthier the society is. Some peoples have a tendency toward property rights, some have hardly shown a conception of it even in the 21st century, and most peoples are somewhere in between.

As parents, we are *stewards* of the bodies of our children. It is our responsibility to render to them, when they become biological adults, the full extent of their property. If we fail in this highest of responsibilities, our children are entitled to seek redress and restitution for the damage we have caused, whether through our aggression, manipulation, or neglect.

Think of it this way: childhood is a voyage. As parents, we are the captains of that voyage and our children are the passengers and the precious cargo. We have been entrusted to see the voyage through and bring the precious cargo to safety at the completion of the journey. Only, the voyage isn't some 15th century *total roll of the dice* across the mighty Atlantic with primitive conceptions of what lies on the other side. Where barbaric tribesmen can hurl spears and arrows and cut us down like dogs when we land on hostile shores. Where horrible winds lash us helplessly and terrible dysentery or scurvy can set in. This is not the Oregon Trail game where everyone drowns in the river or dies of a snake bite. This is the 21st century. The parenting journey is air conditioned with fairly affordable food commodities, full choice in your personal life of who you choose to partner up with, and diaper technology is the best it has ever been. You, as a parent, have unprecedented control over parenting outcomes. That is unless a Democrat becomes President, mandatory fetal tissue-containing vaccines are the norm, and homeschooling is outlawed at the Federal level. But let us proceed like this stuff is not going to happen. Let us focus on what you can do as a conscientious parent with a large degree of control over the home life of your child.

It is important to make the distinction that as a parent, you do not *own* your child. Your child is not a possession. Your child may be an asset but should you choose to develop that asset selfishly and for your own ends, you will reap the neurosis of resentment and rebellion in your child when they become an adult. The majority of parents, particularly in the developing Third World, make the mistake of thinking they own their child. They turn to behavioral control tactics and open, public violence to ensure submission in their children. This is a low and catastrophic way to view one's own responsibilities as a parent. This leads to the Stone Age, where a lot of the world still resides. You do not need to be some *tough* punisher of your child. You need to turn over to your child, when they become biological adults and capable economic or reproductive agents, a fully intact mental and physical body so that they can collaborate with you in doing good works for the world.

Chapter Three: What Peaceful Parenting Is *Not*

It is important from the outset that we understand what is *not* peaceful parenting. Entire, lengthy books, stacks and stacks of them are dedicated to the mistakes that parents make. A few get it right. Most of them talk about how parents are not being liberal enough with their children. Here I will highlight some of the mistakes that parents in America make.

Abuse

People generally react with suspicion, anger, and resistance when traditional parenting methods are questioned. Spanking is the most common. Let us get this one out of the way early on. Spanking has been a mainstay of parenting up until about two decades ago. The response to someone questioning spanking is something along the lines of, "This is how it has been forever. If it ain't broke, don't fix it. I was spanked and I turned out fine!" This is also known as *survivor bias*. This common retort does several things:

-It denies the emotional experience of the child in the moment, especially the first time the child is struck.

-It denies that humans can improve morally.

-It closes people off to the idea that they may not be so "fine". (As if "fine" is a standard to aspire to.)

-It shields previous generations from criticism in order to keep them in an idealized state.

There are two points of modern research that completely detonate any and all justifications for spanking, including the Biblical ones where clever theologians cite this passage and that passage from the Holy Bible as if we are unable to plainly see that Jesus himself did not go around spanking children. These points are as follows:

Spanking is associated with less compliance than other forms of discipline (Gershoff, 2013). Spanking likely doesn't work as a form of punishment, because it causes physical pain, leading to fear and confusion in children, which could, in turn, interfere when the child is trying to learn the rule or message that a parent is attempting to convey (Gershoff, 2013).

Spanking has been linked to increases in negative behaviors, such as physical aggression. In a large meta-analysis of 14 different studies on the effects of spanking on children, researchers found a consistent relationship between spanking and aggressive behavior (Gershoff & Grogan-Kaylor, 2016). On top of leading to more aggressive behavior in children, spanking is also associated with more mental health problems, lower self-esteem, cognitive difficulties, and more negative relationships between children and their parents (Gershoff & Grogan-Kaylor, 2016). Harsh corporal punishment has even been associated with problems in brain development (Tomoda et al., 2009). Yelling, verbal abuse, and shaming have been associated with similar outcomes.[10]

People who resort to the, "I turned out fine!" non-argument simply and most often have not *heard* the facts on spanking. Who sits around thinking to themselves, "I am going to inhibit my child's brain development"? Nobody. Most people are generally good and want to do the right thing. To some degree, we have Western Civilization because Europeans have understood, unlike other barbaric and horrifying cultures and religions, that you ought not to do things like bury your children alive or take child brides. When the average American is exposed to the more extreme side of what passes for "parenting" in the Third World, there is some understanding that this could not fly in the US and that Child Protective Services would need to be called. This is a good start but we can continue to improve our moral condition, both through ethical research and philosophical self-inquiry.

People have such a staunch, hostile reaction when spanking is questioned because it shakes the foundations of their emotional, psychological, and social lives. If they are at all receptive to better arguments here, they begin to think thoughts such as:

-You mean to tell me my parents weren't perfect? That's absurd! They did the best they could! I'm doing the best I can, aren't I?

-I don't have a hardened, unempathetic, and largely uncurious stance toward the inner lives of children, do I?

---

[10] https://www.psychologytoday.com/us/blog/the-baby-scientist/201812/the-science-spanking

-There's no link between the aggression I witnessed as a child and my tolerance and even relish for verbal aggression as an adult, is there?

-There has been no moral improvement for humans in the past centuries because my pastor/imam/rabbi needs to make a strange spectacle about their own private spanking practices, has there?

-Maybe I have been wrong about politics at times because my baseline level of anxiety is high as I became accustomed to being quietly terrified of being punished by authorities larger than myself...

The costs of beginning to consider the arguments and evidence against spanking may be high for a person. To begin to think of spanking as a damaging, trust-breaking behavior perpetrated against children provokes a person's own trauma of being spanked themselves. This is a sensitive issue but it must be addressed in the early going of this book.

Spanking is not without its dangers, even in the "idyllic" form of spanking put forward by defenders of the practice. "My father/mother would tell us what we did wrong in a calm tone and then instruct us gracefully to bend over and then deliberate strikes were placed tastefully on the buttocks and never more than X amount of strikes because that would be inhumane!" is more or less the drift. From *Plain Talk About Spanking*, we read:

> Medical science has long recognized and documented in great detail how being struck on the buttocks can stimulate sexual feelings. Children are especially susceptible. The tragic consequence for many children who have been punished by spanking is that they form a connection between pain, humiliation and sexual arousal that endures for the rest of their lives. In *Slaughter of the Innocents*, David Bakan writes:

"...The buttocks are the locus for the induction of pain in a child. We are familiar with the argument that it is a safe 'locus' for spanking. However, the anal region is also the major erotic region at precisely the time the child is likely to be beaten there. Thus, it is aptly chosen to achieve the result of deranged sexuality in adulthood..." 1971 (p. 113)

The pornography and prostitution industries do a thriving business catering to the needs of countless unfortunate individuals whose sexual development has been derailed by childhood spankings. If we put all other considerations aside, this should be reason enough never to spank a child.

Located deep in the buttocks is the sciatic nerve, the largest nerve in the body. A severe blow to the buttocks, particularly with a blunt instrument, could cause bleeding in the muscles that surround that nerve, possibly injuring it and causing impairment to the involved leg.

In addition to nerve damage and soft tissue damage, a blow to the buttocks can cause injury to the tailbone (coccyx) or sacrum. It sends force waves upward through the spinal column possibly causing disc compression or compression fractures of vertebral bones.

Some people, in their attempt to justify battering children's buttocks, claim that God or nature intended that part of the anatomy for spanking. That claim is brazenly perverse. No part of the human body was made to be mistreated.

NoSpank.net is an authoritative resource on spanking and this author gives the site his highest recommendation. The movement against spanking is not fledgling and discredited. As of 2018, the American

Academy of Pediatrics (AAP) has been recommending that parents do not spank their children at all.

Another objection to anti-spanking is roughly as follows, "Look at the world today! All these young rioters, looters, and murderers don't know any respect. They should have had their asses whooped when they were kids. We have gone soft because we went too soft on the kids when they were growing up." This sort of opinion is at least indicative that *something* went wrong in the parenting of America's current young generations. But some violent mindset of moral outrage at Twitter videos is not rigorous thinking at all. What did go wrong with the Millennial generation, as mentioned earlier, is that daycare rates peaked in the 1990's and early 2000's. More than ever, America turned her young children out of the home and into the care of strangers so that the parents could be caffeinated and engaged in the work of making corporations rich. The effect this had was to expose middle class aspirants to a socialist education curriculum, the barbarity of Third World fostering techniques at the daycares, and sever the connection between parents and children that nurtures a moral conscience. America turned her children over to liberal public-school teachers, low rent foreigner nannies and $9 an hour parent figures at the daycares, and the cope for all of this was mass entertainment. Enjoy a weekend full of media indoctrination. They are sure to teach your kids about the value of productive enterprise, social order, and the total primacy of the institution of free speech, right? America soured after the Marxist revolution of the swinging 1960's and few are willing to take ownership. Taking ownership in the home is the place to start, not hurling invective on social media in the hopes that some ANTIFA punks will have their feelings hurt and somehow realize that their parents were "soft" on them. If anything, constant neglect and being pawned off to non-relatives in order to chase the few career opportunities the central banks cough out is *rather hard* on children and young people. Pile spanking on top of that and you have a mob of failed middle class aspirants who have neither the ability to articulate value in what is left of a Western economy nor the interest in helping others to do so. People have a need to recreate the emotional desolation of their childhoods. That is why we see American cities on fire.

Spanking has proven deleterious effects on the health of a child. Professor Murray Straus of the University of New Hampshire conducted a groundbreaking study on the matter:

> Straus found that children in the United States who were spanked had lower IQs four years later than those who were not spanked.

> Straus and Mallie Paschall, senior research scientist at the Pacific Institute for Research and Evaluation, studied nationally representative samples of 806 children ages 2 to 4, and 704 ages 5 to 9. Both groups were retested four years later.

> IQs of children ages 2 to 4 who were not spanked were 5 points higher four years later than the IQs of those who were spanked. The IQs of children ages 5 to 9 years old who were not spanked were 2.8 points higher four years later than the IQs of children the same age who were spanked.

> 'How often parents spanked made a difference. The more spanking the, the slower the development of the child's mental ability. But even small amounts of spanking made a difference,' Straus says.

Straus is considered the national expert on the subject. Corporal punishment is extremely stressful to the child and becomes a chronic stressor to those who experience it on a regular basis. The average frequency of corporal punishment is three to four times a week. Children who are spanked develop fears that terrible things are about to happen and an increase in being easily startled. These are both symptoms associated with lower IQ. There is also a strong correlation between national IQ and spanking:

> Straus also found a lower national average IQ in nations in which spanking was more prevalent. His analysis indicates the strongest link between corporal punishment and IQ was for those whose parents continued to use corporal punishment even when they were teenagers.
>
> Straus and colleagues in 32 nations used data on corporal punishment experienced by 17,404 university students when they were children.[11]

In developed nations, spanking is a dirty secret that has no presence in the corporate media. It flies under the radar because there is a collective acknowledgement that the practice is *wrong* at its most fundamental level. You are more likely to see the sexualization of children in media in today's media environment than you are to see spanking. Spanking is too close to home for most people. Nothing good comes from it. Depicting it in media would arouse primal, agonizing feelings in the viewers. Attitudes about spanking over time have soured, "The pro-spanking bloc has slipped from about 84 percent in 1986 to about 70 percent in 2010 and 2012. That's still a majority, but spanking has become less socially acceptable over the past three decades.[12]" The sentiment that spanking has no place in parenting is not a cure-all. There are countries with high spanking rates that have high national IQ's (but no gun rights and no free speech). There are people who were spanked who have achieved plenty in life. Some of them even used their having been spanked as fuel for

---

[11] https://www.sciencedaily.com/releases/2009/09/090924231749.htm
[12] https://fivethirtyeight.com/features/americans-opinions-on-spanking-vary-by-party-race-region-and-religion/

motivation to achieve but these people were likely to have been exceptional either way. These people and nations are *exceptions*. The majority of people spanked never make it out of emotional childhood.

Let us have a look at some of the other common mistakes that parents make.

The three main categories of parental failure are aggression, manipulation, and neglect. Aside from physical aggression, which most commonly takes the form of spanking, we have verbal aggression. Verbal aggression also strays into the category of manipulation but it primarily consists of the following:

-yelling

-name calling and insults

-growling and intimidation

-criticism

-attacking others in the presence of the child, including fighting with the spouse

Verbal aggression follows the line of "might makes right", only fists, kicks, and open palms are not used. Verbal aggression intimidates the child into silence and obedience. Fathers bellow and mothers shriek. Neither is appropriate and neither fosters the reasoning capacities of the child. Attacking others in front of the child, such as an older sibling or even a stranger out in the world, dictates to the child that the same will happen to them if they are out of line. We are entering an age where families, not the police, will be more and more in charge of their own defense and so notable exceptions include situations where the family is attacked unjustly and the parents must defend. We do not fault American settlers for having a terse word or an explosive showdown with the marauding tribes of Indians looking for horses to steal and children to rape. Our situation is becoming like theirs. Barbarism is once again threatening to derail our settlements.

Verbal aggression gives your kid a complex:

> Exposure to parental verbal aggression has been shown to exert enduring adverse psychiatric effects, comparable in magnitude to other forms of childhood adversity such as witnessing domestic violence and extra- familial sexual abuse (Teicher, Samson, Polcari, & McGreenery, 2006). Johnson et al. (2001) found evidence that individuals who experienced maternal verbal aggression during childhood were more than 3 times as likely as those who did not to have borderline, narcissistic, obsessive-compulsive, and paranoid personality disorders during adolescence or early adulthood.[13]

There are near infinite parenting blogs out there that have listicles along the lines of "5 Ways To Deal With Your Child's Aggressive Behavior" and basically all of them suggest you engage behavior modification techniques with your kid. It is next to impossible to find one that tells you to reflect upon your own behavior and your own aggression. Bob says to Jim, "Jim, why is my kid such a prick?" to which Jim responds, "Look in the mirror, pal." It is as simple as that with verbal aggression. Madness is not heritable. Madness is passed intergenerationally through learned behavior. You blow your top because your mom or dad blew their tops because their parents blew their tops.

The line with verbal aggression between adults is less distinct than it is between an adult and a child. With adults, especially men, there

---

[13] https://www.ncbi.nlm.nih.gov/pmc/articles/PMC3946237/

is a lot of verbal jockeying and jousting. Men stoke competitive fires in one another with verbal pressure and sparring, as I wrote in *Dead West Walking: Masculine Values and Survival Principles for The Decline*[14]. To some degree, men can test each other in a way that is not always appropriate between parent and child. Sometimes they cajole one another back into the fraternal order. Men (and women nowadays) are often political opponents. They accuse each other of trespasses, give each other insulting names, and take each other by surprise to gain an advantage. In principled conservatives, these are not indicators of abuse as the boundaries of politics or male to male adult friendships are not the same as the parent-child relationship. With adult male friendships and mentorships, it is still important that a spirit of collaboration, encouragement, and moral improvement be adopted so that terse moments where a harsh word or even a disciplining is an unusual occurrence that serves to take the situation out of high stakes and back in to lower stakes. Who would fault a man for ripping the steering wheel away from his buddy if his buddy were driving drunk? Who would fault a man for calling his buddy a simp for falling under the spell of a witchy woman? Only evil people would! Damaged, problematic people have not earned completely exemplary treatment from everyone they come into contact to. We are all, to a degree, undergoing a refining and civilizing process in our social and business lives, unless we have succumbed to nihilism and childhood despair. Hardcore feminists and Marxist activists seek to elicit violent containment from moral people. It is not verbal or physical abuse to oblige them. A software executive who picks his nose until it bleeds at boardroom meetings may be growled at by a superior and no verbal abuse has come to pass. With adult relationships, the standards take into account reciprocity in a way that the parent-child relationship does not. Children are owed exemplary parenting from their

---

[14] https://www.amazon.com/Dead-West-Walking-Masculine-Principles-ebook/dp/B07S4K7PMZ

parents because they come into the world innocent. Adults are due whatever they have accrued in their adult personal and business relationships.

With an eye on how parents trespass against their children, let us have a look at some of the verbally abusive behaviors laid out by Healthline[15]:

> **"They insult or attempt to humiliate you. Then they accuse you of being overly sensitive or say that it was a joke and you have no sense of humor."**

This is a particularly cruel behavior because a child's own sensitivity is used against them. Children know what is funny: novel associations that push dialogue forward in quality. Insulting a child is not funny. Insulting an adult can be funny if they are an immoral actor and the insult garners consensus against the trespasses of the person.

> **"They frequently yell or scream at you."**

Physical violence is the surest sign a person has lost the argument. People "lose the argument' with their children all the time and resort to demeaning their children to maintain control. Yelling or screaming at a child is the same. There are outlier situations, like raising your voice over traffic so the kid will not toddle out into it in the moment you have looked away or humming loudly into the ear of a colicky child, but let us face it: these situations are few and far between.

> **"The initial disagreement sets off a string of accusations and dredging up of unrelated issues to put you on the defense."**

---

[15] https://www.healthline.com/health/mental-health/what-is-verbal-abuse

Parents sometimes harbor resentment against their children. This happens when the parent fails to take fully into account the responsibilities associated with raising a child. A parent will be upset that the kid broke something, that the kid cost money, that the kid soiled themselves, that the kid hid something out of fear, and so forth. Then the parent will bring this out in a fight later as evidence that the child is wrong somehow. Children are not moral agents. They become moral agents when they can earn a full-time living for themselves, which is somewhere around age sixteen. People who feel resentment toward their children need to help themselves more comprehensively master the responsibilities associated with raising their children. The answer to situations that are a "drag" is to be more proactively engaged in the child's life.

"They try to make you feel guilty and position themselves as the victim."

A parent is never the victim of the child. Yes, children "steal" money from their parents. Yes, children are violent with their parents. Children can say something nasty to their parents. All of this is learned behavior. The parents chose to have the child.

"They save their hurtful behaviors for when you're alone but act completely different when others are around."

This is an insidious aspect of bad parenting. It makes child abuse harder to detect for the community around the child. Children are not exactly capable and ready advocates of peaceful parenting techniques. They derive their moral awareness from their parents. If their parents are involved in covert abuse, the child's personality splits as the child learns to have one mindset when the parents are around and another when the family is in public or around others. The true measure of a person is how they treat children and animals when they are alone with them. Covert abusers can get away with what they do for years and years. A lot of the danger of "social distancing" is that the social fabric is thinned and there is far less accountability built in to communities. This author was surprised once to see a clip from a show where a set of parents lived in the far interior of Alaska sixty miles from any settlement with their teenage boy. They openly grew marijuana plants and it was obvious that the son was a pot smoker. Another story about social distancing permitting abuse to go unchecked comes out of Alaska, "Alaska's hands-off approach to independent home schooling, among the most relaxed in the country, was suddenly in the spotlight last week amid news reports of two teenagers who showed up at the Covenant House on Christmas Eve 2015 and the filing of neglect charges against their parents. The girls, then ages 16 and 17, said their parents had forced them to live in the basement without heat or water. They never attended public school and had very little home schooling from their mother, according to a charging document written by an Anchorage police detective. The detective said that when he interviewed the girls, they didn't have the normal skills of children their age, which he attributed to their lack of "socialization and education."[16] Social distancing, a form of social isolation, feeds neglect and the more extreme levels of child abuse. There is nothing wrong with living somewhere quite rural but to use it as a smokescreen of your mistreatment of your kids *is* wrong.

Though child abuse is down because families are more intact during government lockdowns, the severity of child abuse cases

---

[16] https://www.adn.com/education/article/alaska-has-one-country-s-loosest-homeschooling-laws/2016/05/09/

that do come in has increased, "That's when Dr. Norrell Atkinson, section chief of the child protection program at St. Christopher's Hospital for Children in Philadelphia, started noticing a change. She's a child abuse pediatrician at the 180-bed hospital, which is affiliated with the medical schools at Drexel and Temple universities. The hospital is a Level 1 trauma and burn center that tends to treat more severely injured kids anyway, but there has been a noticeable change lately. 'Numbers are down overall, but we're tending to see kids that are more severely injured,' she said. 'We are seeing more kids coming into the ER with more severe injuries that require hospitalization.'[17] The unintended effect of closing the public schools down is that families are more together. The downside of this, as a social subsidy has been rapidly torn away like a suture, is that the release valve of kids going to school the next day after a bad night of parenting is gone. Conflict in the homes of mentally unstable, criminally disturbed parents is going unchecked for longer periods of time. Schooling programs have been a lifeline for severely abused children.

"They get into your personal space or block you from moving away."

This fits more accurately with the physical abuse side of the aggression category. All people need personal space to process their feelings and make up their minds. This is particularly true of Western Civilization, an order founded by reflective people who valued Christian prayer and silence. These are salves for social ills. Social ills in the family require boundaries, reflection, and contemplation – especially by the parents. The parent fails to

---

[17] https://www.usatoday.com/story/news/nation/2020/05/13/hospitals-seeing-more-severe-child-abuse-injuries-during-coronavirus/3116395001/

lead this example when he or she invades the personal space of the child. As children maturate, they need their own "owned space" to retreat from the world to – even absent any situation of abuse. Parents who are invasive against their children are a dime a dozen. Many do it because the conflict with the child has provoked ancient feelings of powerlessness in them that they then project onto the child so as to justify dominating the child. "This child is powerless and I am going to *make* them know it, by golly!" is roughly the justification. The parent who harbors feelings of powerlessness is the one who is provoked and upset by resistance or disagreement from the child. Children are free to disagree. Disagreement is an opportunity to come closer. The parent figure who attempts to broach *intimacy* with the child, as opposed to domination, is the parent who respects the autonomy of the child. Nobody in their right mind wants to be chased, especially innocent children.

Criticism is also a pernicious kind of verbal abuse. Criticism is an unfavorable or critical observation or remark. Criticism is a conclusion about a person, such as, "You are naughty for pooping your pants" or "You are gross for touching your private parts, as a toddler." People commonly think that criticism is what made them excellent but children can be given a knowledge of what is incorrect behavior without remarks after the fact, which comprises the majority of criticism from parents. We want to be proactive with children, not reactive and critical after the fact. Most people have a quasi-sociopathic relationship to criticism: they think it is supposed to be doled out freely in personal relationships to make others better and if outsiders criticize them they just harden up until the criticism goes away. Criticism does not breed excellence. Children succeed *despite* criticism. Criticism instills doubt and neuroticism in children. Because of parental criticism, children loathe themselves for farting, feel ashamed for having bathroom accidents, feel downhearted for not living up to the example of an older sibling, and a million other variations.

Children are developing people filled with curiosity, creativity, empiricism, and an earnest desire to do right and help others out. Parents who put negative conclusions or criticisms on children are behaving in an abusive manner and need to remind themselves of the wonder of their child. Criticism does not make children "tough". It makes them numb their true feelings. Criticism is a valid tool of containment against objectively bad political actors but in the hands of a parent, it becomes a homewrecking bludgeon. Worse yet is when parents collude to criticize a child. They often do this by muttering in low voices to one another from another room, voicing their complaints and frustrations with their child. Children are not frustrating because their wonder always outshines their rougher sides that need our civilizing refinement. Yes, parents are allowed to feel frustrated but complaining about a child is not appropriate behavior. Rather, the frustration needs to be *processed* appropriately with a collaborative, positive attitude aimed at training and mediation – not punishment and whining.

A lot of parents justify criticizing their children by saying, "It's a tough world out there and if I don't toughen up my child through criticism, they are in for a *harsh reality* when they're older." Peaceful parenting is a language of negotiation, empiricism, assertion, and reasoning. When bad actors in the broader world engage a child that has been peacefully parented, the child is simply in touch with their true feelings toward the bad actor – anger, annoyance, impatience, or disgust. What is more disarming against a verbal abuser, being told, "When you do x, y, z, I feel disgusted and want you to stop" or some strange psychological transference because the verbal abuser's victim feels the need to out-criticize the criticizer? People who were criticized in childhood fall in with other people who were criticized in childhood and *evil people run the world*. Sure, some people who were criticized in childhood end up running things in adulthood but more often than not, people who were criticized in childhood develop self-worth issues and turn to substance abuse in adulthood that limits their socio-economic advancement. For every one person who got "thick skin" from their parents, there are a million and one neurotics (usually liberals) who cannot function properly as value producers in society. Why take the risk? Beyond this, the toughest kids are the ones who know what their dream in life is and are highly organized, meaning making venturers fully equipped to *deliver* on life's promise. The people who get ahead furthest in business, the real world of human development (not government), are people who were stewarded responsibly by their businesspeople parents, maybe got a loan to get started, and are millionaires while the mass of people are still slaving away at college degrees. The real head start in life is being parented well, not having verbal blows rained down upon you so you will rhetorically beat the daylights out of people you get fixated upon in the broader world because their dysfunctions remind you of your own.

Some families have criticism as the entire basis of communication with one another. We commonly understand that these people live in trailer parks, the ghetto, or the projects. These are families where bickering is ever present, dysfunction is rampant, and there is little hope for any kind of improvement absent outside intervention. We understand that these people are at the extreme end of the spectrum of criticism. There is no "golden mean" with criticism because criticism is fundamentally wrong. We do not go around saying that there is a golden mean with heroin use or spanking. "If I only spank this kid one time a year, he will become a captain of industry," is not a thought that crosses people's minds. Wrong is wrong. Criticism is wrong. It is a tool of vain or insecure parents who need to control their children's behavior because their children shine too brightly, feel too intensely, scream and squeal too loudly, and provoke what amounts to PTSD in the parent from the parent's own mistreatment via criticism long ago. If a kid poops their pants, they are not a pants-pooper you need to be bitter about. Just explain how the toilet works, even if it is the two-hundredth time. Using the toilet is an acquired art, not a first instinct.

Manipulation is the second worst category of abuse, after neglect, because it actively distorts and warps a child's moral and ideological bases. Physical aggression does so to a degree but it is overt and the easiest of the three to process, generally speaking. Manipulation is when the parent misinforms the child in order to cope with his own difficult internal states. We see a lot of this today in the media with parents twisting their children against President Trump when no President in US history has done more than Trump to battle the scourge of child trafficking that Obama and Bush Jr. allowed to fester. These parents put their children on parade with signs that the children did not make. They indoctrinate their children with hateful, anti-white ideologies. Their children become political pawns instead of innocent adventure-seekers who need protection from the madness of the world outside of the home. Manipulation takes many forms. Too many to list here but I will list a cursory top ten:

1) Complaining to the child about the other parent

This is wrong because the parents needed to have sorted their disagreements on values *before* they had children in order to be consonant in parenting styles. This undermines the harmony of the home, teaches the child disloyalty, and usually injects the child with some measure of distrust for the opposite sex. There is little to no conflict in the home between parents who have been self-knowledgeable and raised well themselves. Where there *is* conflict, there needs to be clear principles of de-escalation for communication and problem solving.

2) Intoxicating the child with media in order to avoid emotional vulnerability

People with sparse or fractured inner lives generally need media to dictate their identities to them and to keep them distracted from the oftentimes painful and difficult work of maturing into a real adult. Children are meaning-making machines, in a sense, as they are constantly curious and seeking out novelty in order to leverage into new concepts. Manipulative and especially neglectful parents take advantage of this fact by exposing their children to media devices so that time will pass and all parties involved can feel as if something "was had". The truth is that, aside from its utility as a communication device with other people through messaging, there is scant little for a child to gain from media and the downsides are legion. Children need fables, moral stories (like from the Holy Bible), and direct contact with others. Video games and movies are a distant second best yet so many hundreds of millions of parents settle because they would rather not rock the boat and disturb the bounds of our bored, socialist societies. These uninspired parents feel relief when they see their child gob smacked by the same media that once hypnotized them. The truth is that children benefit from their parents to the degree that their parents are emotionally and existentially engaged with their development. A simple fishing trip or a couple hours in the park are worth more than a week's worth of sitting together or separately in front of media devices. Teach your child a single song to sing. It's worth more than all the Marvel movies combined!

3) Imposing unnatural "gender identities" on the child

Boys are boyish. Girls are girlish. They come out of the womb this way. They are distinct. They exhibit these natural, hard engrained differences before they are done with breastfeeding. Girls are gentle and nurturing. Boys growl, grunt, and tussle. Girls like to help their mothers take care of the other kids or farm animals. Boys follow their fathers around and get into whatever papa is doing. There are rare exceptions to these tendencies and they are ideologically blown out of proportions so that insecure parents can manage in themselves how difficult it is for them to tolerate that there is a little being in their care that exhibits natural gender roles more adequately than they do. Little infants are not confused about what they are. They simply follow their natural cues that pull them into being grown men or women, depending on the sex they are born with. Incest comes into play when daddy only had girls and wanted a boy or mommy wanted more girls, or whatever. People put their problems on their children. This is wrong. There is no such thing as a transgender child. This is an invention brought on by massively available Internet pornography and the corporate welfare state.

A child will sometimes experiment with gender-inappropriate play. A girl will want to be like her dad. She feels emotionally distant from him, because he works too hard or did not want a girl in the first place, and so to capture his attention and affection will show an unnatural interest in his tools, his cars, or whatever else has displaced his connection from her. Gender-inappropriate play on the part of the child is the sign that the parent of the opposite sex must intervene to improve their connection with the child. The parent stokes the child's self-knowledge during this corrective process by explaining to the child what the child's natural roles are. The child is redirected to her natural interests with a more secure knowledge of them and she learns that there are things that boys do that she is not expected to do in order to win approval or satisfaction from her father. She learns that mothers are more inclined to their daughters, as mothers do not separate from their daughters until their daughters are married, and that fathers are inclined to their sons because they need sons or sons-in-law to pass their productive enterprises off to. When a child knows the essentials of natural gender roles and their value, she takes to developing in herself the qualities that will best permit her to succeed as an adult. A child *only* benefits from having his or her natural, biological gender roles (as derived from traditional knowledge) reflected back from the correct parent. A mother will struggle to teach her sons how to be men and fathers. A man will have difficulties teaching his daughters how to be women and mothers.

No, girls do not get to play with tools and trucks. No, boys do not get to play with dolls and dresses. Parents who encourage this are perverts and confused themselves. Boys do not need to play with girl toys in order to empathize with girls more and vice versa. This is a fantasy put forward by bored, liberal white women who have daddy issues. Boys and girls do not need to be integrated to get along better later. In fact, the opposite is true. There is more respect between men and women who were raised distinctly and largely separately, in boys or girls schools in ages past.

Giving boys girl toys is especially harmful. So much of what is male in our current society is being taken away from men. Giving boys girl toys starts this programming early. A boy's maleness has become something to overlook. For girls to see boys playing with girl toys and to be presented with boy toys themselves presents them with the feminist notion that there is no difference between boys and girls. This bigotry teaches girls not to trust men's leadership later on in adulthood.

These is nothing whatsoever abusive about discouraging boys from playing with girl toys and the inverse. Discouragement is not abusive, in and of itself. There are natural delineations in our gender roles. Discouragement that helps a child to learn these boundaries over time is good parenting. We do not want to be shaming when we discourage our children from harmful behaviors. A tone of assertive correction is sufficient. Gentle, early correction spares our children painful confusion down the line – which is pounced upon by the sickos wrecking the world.

We also want to dress our children appropriately by choosing masculine colors for our boys to wear and pretty colors for our girls to wear. Boys do not get to wear dresses. Girls wear blue jeans, overalls, and t-shirts much less often than boys – if at all.

4)   Teasing the child to undermine his confidence

Insecure parents cannot tolerate when their child exceeds them in any capacity. Intergenerational improvement is a perfectly natural, acceptable occurrence. Barring severe abuse in infancy (such as is common in the Third World), toddlers are *always* less depressed than their parents. Insecure parents bring the child down, instead of boosting themselves up by continuing to endeavor being self-knowledgeable and more morally excellent. Teasing is one of the easiest ways to bring a child down. Make a comment on the child's appearance. Poke fun of a blip in their learning process. Compare them to other children and then laugh. Put your feelings of inadequacy on the child rather than see the obvious: there is a tremendously high chance this kid will exceed you in most things and you are going to bestow all your wealth on the kid when you are an old fart. Easier to negate their progress with biting little comments so you do not have to take a deep breath and chill for once in your life, right? Get outta here! No more teasing.

5)   Sexualizing the child with an inappropriate look or touch or instructing the child to "experiment"

People who have not had their romantic love needs met, by first falling in love with their own artistry and enterprise and then finding a person of the opposite sex who reflects this back to them, are in a state of childishness. They need sexual gratification to feel better about their condition. When these people become parents, they do all sorts of weird things to their kids. The most common is emotional incest. You have probably heard of daddy's little girlfriend or mommy's little man. It happens all the time. Children do not exist for the sexual or romantic gratification of adults. Children have their own independent learning process and the boundaries of this process must be respected. Introducing sexualization turns the child into an object of gratification. Past infancy, walking around naked in front of a child of the opposite sex over-involves the child in their natural curiosity about bodily organs and they will seek to experiment with children of the opposite sex when they are older. This leads to early sexual activity, which cripples a child's ability to have innocent love as a teenager and young adult (which is one of the sweetest things in life).

On the opposite end of the spectrum, there are parents who castigate and shame children for touching their own body parts. You can gently discourage a child from playing with their genitals. You do not need to make it a neurosis. The same way a shepherd whistles or does a brief call to redirect the flock, so can the sturdy but gentle guidance of a parent operate. Girls will want to hold hands with boys. Boys will want to kiss girls on the cheek. Some measure of this serves the child in their natural learning and growing process. Parents must not *control* outcomes after the fact but instill values so that good choices on the part of the child compound. An asexual child has been failed by their parents almost as much as a promiscuous child has been failed by sexualized attention. There is nothing wrong with prudeness in a child, so long as the child is not inhibited from being competitive or daring.

Parents need to remember that sexual energy can be turned into creative and morally courageous energy. Sexuality does not operate in some kind of wholly separate chamber that needs to be constantly monitored for disruptions. Teach the child to integrate their sexuality into virtuous pursuits. Do this for yourself.

Another of the most common ways a child is sexualized is through exposure to pornography. The average age of exposure to pornography is 11 years old[18] and children under the age of 10 account for 22% of online porn consumption under 18-years old.[19] Pornography is rampant in America. Indecency laws were struck down by a hostile elite and libertine judiciary and now the average person finds himself inundated by pornographic images to a degree that would shock post-WWI Berliners. This author was on a plane flight with a major airline just this past weekend and looked up to see an explicit sex scene playing out on the LCD screen of the person two rows ahead. The top song on the pop charts features the explicit lyrics, "Hop on top, I wanna ride. I do a Kegel while it's inside. Spit in my mouth, look in my eyes. This p*ssy is wet, come take a dive." Since indecency cannot be criminally prosecuted and pornographers cannot be jailed, America has become a smut show. The children are ground down by this. They lose their capacity for pair bonding as they are drawn into a world of promiscuous sex, vapid consumption, gender bending, and recreational drugs. Children should not be accessing the Internet, at all. Pornography is even in children's shows. There is too much widespread smut on the Internet for a child to be able to go online without coming into contact with it. Until the moral conversation at the heart of America changes and our laws are severely overhauled, children need to remain offline or in tightly controlled online environments with active porn blocking software and for only limited periods of time as digital media itself has a degrading and distracting effect on children's mental faculties.

Children who go to public are not protected from the Internet. Children do not have a need to be on social media as they are not economic agents providing for families. Children should not be displayed in images on social media, no matter how wholesome the parent thinks their content is. A parent needs to think about how many pedophiles are

---

[18] https://www.breakthecycle.org/talking-your-child-about-pornography-0
[19] https://www.netnanny.com/blog/the-detrimental-effects-of-pornography-on-small-children/

out there, masturbating to their children's images before taking what they think is a righteous stand by promoting their content using their own children. Your children are not an accessory for your business enterprise in this age of the Internet. Children are not celebrities. This is not an appropriate role. This role only exists because of Satanic pedophile directors and producers in Hollywood. Remember, the very first child "star" was Shirley Temple, who was exposed to a producer's penis when she was 12 years old.[20] Photographs and images of your children are for private circulation in your immediate family and for grandparents. Perhaps when Satanic pedophile elite are not at the helm of society and most certainly at the helm of Big Tech will it be safe to post pictures of one's own children on the Internet but what is there to be gained anyway. Children do not exist so that one can improve one's own image in the eyes of others. Children are not a marketing tool.

One other way children are sexualized is through the inappropriate sexual activities of parents in front of their children. A passionate kiss here and there or a loving embrace is no problem. When physical intimacy moves from the romantic and into the sexual is where the line for appropriateness is drawn. Parents should not engage in sex acts in front of their children. There should be no undressing, fondling, groping, petting, or French kissing. When a child sees this, they seek to emulate it as they do with all things their parents do. This leads to inappropriate early childhood experiences. When parents engage in sex acts with one another in front of the children, they enlist the children as participants because children have no conception of holding boundaries with their parents. Beyond this, it is wrong for parents to have sex in front of their children because this robs children of the innocence they need to be able to put up an effective effort later on in not having pre-marital sex as teenagers and adults. Children must suspend their disgust reflex in

---

[20] https://www.newsweek.com/old-hollywood-starlets-endured-sexual-harassment-weinstein-effect-710885

order to normalize their parents' voyeuristic sexual activities. They then have difficulties identifying later in life what public acts are indecent and they also choose slimy, boundaryless partners.

According to the National Center for Victims of Crime:

-1 in 5 girls and 1 in 20 boys is a victim of child sexual abuse;

-Self-report studies show that 20% of adult females and 5-10% of adult males recall a childhood sexual assault or sexual abuse incident;

-During a one-year period in the U.S., 16% of youth ages 14 to 17 had been sexually victimized;

-Over the course of their lifetime, 28% of U.S. youth ages 14 to 17 had been sexually victimized;

-Children are most vulnerable to CSA between the ages of 7 and 13

Sexual assault is both manipulation and aggression, two of the major categories of childhood abuse. Sexual assault is an epidemic in the black American community, with some studies showing that up to 50% of all black girls in the United States being victims of sexual assault and the vast majority being assaulted by males of their own community. Sexual abuse fills children with a sense of self-loathing and shame. Profound dissociation sets in. The child's very personhood is violated. People who were sexually assaulted in childhood struggle the rest of their lives to attain a sense of normalcy. One study showed that 32% of survivors of childhood sexual assault had attempted suicide at some point.[21]

---

[21] https://pubmed.ncbi.nlm.nih.gov/11888413/

At no point is it *ever* appropriate for a parent to make physical or verbal sexual advances upon their child. Some perverted parents will try to skirt this by looking upon their sons and daughters with sexual desire. This is deeply hurtful to the child as it is a betrayal of the worst order. Children who endure lustful parents will, later in life, seek out authority figures to sexually gratify. These children grow up to use their bodies as commodities, some of them going on to appear in pornography. Even more perverse dynamics can open up as the child can learn that he or she wields sexual power over their parent and will learn a life strategy of flirting with powerful people in order to garner personal favors.

Children are not for the fulfillment of romantic desires of adults. Adults who are attracted to children disrupt the social order more than anyone else and the more intelligent of them develop the most complex power schemes possible in order to cover up their predations. These people were sexualized, molested, or even raped in childhood. They seek to reconnect with the child they once were since they were massively estranged from themselves when they were wounded. They see children as a distant, elusive ideal and their feelings of revenge against their own perpetrators come into the mix, leading to the worst of society's crimes. There is no reason under the sun ever, despite whatever clever emergency ethics scenarios people's twisted minds can come up with, for an adult to have sexual interaction with a child. The West is different from the rest of the world because here we treat sex as sacred. Even atheists, who are self-knowledgeable, are able to understand that a person gives something fundamental about oneself to another with the sex act. This is not to be treated lightly. Adults who sexualize children *steal* from the child. It is extremely difficult and requires years of therapy to recover from sexual abuse experienced in childhood. A young adult more readily recovers from being cattle-branded several times in the face than from being used as a romantic plaything for a pedophile. When pedophiles go to prison, they are rightly targeted for death by heterosexuals and sometimes even homosexuals. It is only because of the liberal world order that pedophiles live among us openly. The liberal world order, at most, concerns itself with the "rehabilitation" of pedophiles instead of with the protection of children. The abuser becomes the aggrieved. The legal age of consent continues to be lowered so that immigrants from actual rape cultures can continue to attack nieces, nephews, and cousins in their vicinity.

Children do not need to "experiment" with sexuality, as liberal so-called experts contend. Sex is the easiest, most simple behavior in the history of the world – aside from eating and breathing. Children need to have a soulful connection with their parents so that when they come of age for courtship with peers of the opposite sex, they will be satisfied in marriage and domestic arrangements irrespective of any "learning" process that goes on with the sex act. They will know to differentiate between the attractions of heartful, conversational relationships and the easy, stupid philandering of the left.

6) Inculcating the child with the anti-heroic, male-hating culture of the left

Children are not natural liberals. Children are born wary of outgroups. Children are born identifying with people who look like them. Children see men as titanic heroes and thirst for heroism and adventure. The left, through liberalism, attacks these naturally occurring sentiments. The culture of the left is massively available, thanks to the Internet and leftist schemes to use government to propagate the Internet as widely as possible through subsidy programs. All of the major media outlets pump out unnatural, toxically feminine themes and messages in order to indoctrinate people in the death cult of worldwide Communism. Exposing a child to this messaging is wrong.

The heroic male, in particular, is a threat to the left. The left is fragile and depends on manipulation to continue its predations. The left derives its power from financial instruments, media power, and the cheap butchery of the mob. The left's worst nightmare is a strong male who can get a high Kill Death Assist ratio (KDA) in defense of the nation. Long gone are the days where stories of the heroic actions of men who earned the Medal of Honor populated the pages of our publications.

The heroic male is important to Western Civilization both because of the hero's journey, which is the prevailing and guiding spirit of all classical education of young European men, but also because the heroic male is the only group that can destroy the left. Communism is fundamentally anti-male. Only fraternal bonds between men can overcome all this moral rot. As such, according to the left, men, and boys in particular, must be kept from one another and prevented from forming coalitions. Too many men pointed in one political direction has always been a mortal danger to the banking elite, so women must be brought in.... women who are corrupt and will do plenty of corrupting wherever they go. If boys can be convinced to self-attack and withhold themselves from the fraternal order, they will not cause political and social troubles later in life. When good men work in tandem, they explore broader horizons than are currently permitted by the homosexual banking order that threatens to ruin everything in an explosion of race war, civil war, and sectarian conflict.

7) Spooking the child with scare stories or tales of suffering that the child cannot process

"Scared straight" is a fairly common parenting style in the United States. The logic follows that if the child can be made terrified enough of doing something wrong, they won't do it. When you introduce fear to a child, it may result in compliance but ultimately the fear will show up in other places. The child's confidence will be hurt or he will be paralyzed in situations where he needs to overcome fear. A lot of kids who are "scared straight" by their parents rebel when they are out of the home and engage in the taboo behavior they were warned away from. The message they took from their parents animation and excitement over a particular behavior was that their parents were animated and excited about it! When you introduce aggression and manipulation, children are less and less able to process the truth value of what is being said. They are put further and further into their limbic system stress response. They shut down. Conveying that a particular behavior is not good for them, while they are in this state, is counterproductive yet it happens in common parenting all the time.

Another problem associated with this mistake in parenting is that using the suffering of someone else as a teaching tool teaches the child, mostly in an unintended way, that the path of suffering is one that offers many lessons. The term "meaningful suffering" gets thrown around a lot if counseling and psychology circles. There is a lot of talk about the nobility of self-denial and the worse the pain, the more noble one is being. This is a non-European take on Christianity. The real question to put to children is *who* is imposing the suffering and for what reasons. This opens up a dialogue about morality, moral agents, and the mentality of people who think they need to impose suffering on others. The child learns to understand criminality and manipulation. Bad parents do not want to have this conversation because it shines a light on their own trespasses and the nature of their trespasses. There are predators in the world and they are imposing suffering. Pain is a natural part of life but the way suffering is used as a "learning" tool for man's fallen nature is simply a way to inflict suffering on a child. Spooking a child with tales of suffering is not something they are generally able to process. Mostly they take away the idea that they should involve themselves in suffering somehow later on in life and they usually do this by saying brutal things to themselves in their private thoughts as teenagers. You do not need stories about misfortune in order to teach a child logical rigor. There is no need to put a child on a path of suffering. It is their choice whether they want to suffer or not. Suffering comes from not living honest values or because some moral aggressor has decided to attack you. Suffering itself is not a learning tool. The moral causality that leads to suffering *is*.

Some parents use the "you're going to end up like so-and-so!" tactic to discourage certain behaviors in their children. This is false certainty. While it is important to understand what is immoral and what is productive behavior, it is a way of locking in a child's perspective by tethering them to some undesirable figure due to no fault of their own. Parents bring up "so-and-so" as a bad example because they have *bad people* in their lives. A highly successful, moral person has a plethora of good examples to inspire their children by and a near total absence of bad people to warn their children about. When you explain *why* people adopt bad behaviors that lead them to become bums, addicts, gamblers, simps, etc., children learn quickly and are free of a sense of impending doom that they will become something unworthy of love in their parents eyes.

8) Comparing oneself to the child as a compensation for low inner self-worth

Some comparison, as a benevolent teaching tool, is useful to a child but it must always be done as a means to inspire and encourage a child. It is alright for a parent to feel insecure from time to time. We are all human. But it is not right for a parent to act out that insecurity by putting their child down. Anything from subtle digs to insults and nitpicking is wrong. Comparing oneself to a child as a compensation of low inner self-worth is an admission of emotional maturity. We used to see this in liberal comedy movies where adults throw tantrums and only experience the consequences a child would, which is unrealistic. In the real world, arrested development is annoying to be around. We accept some degree of it in children because children mature at different rates but it is inappropriate behavior in adults. When a parent compares themselves in an insecure manner to their child, the child experiences pressure to underperform or overperform to buoy the parent's self-esteem. This leads to chronic striving or indigence in adulthood, neither which is a sustainable strategy for laying the groundwork to become a parent oneself. The modern economy does reward chronic striving and work addiction but the family does not.

Comparison to the child as a compensation for low inner self-worth also has the effect of strangling off a kid's engagement in their own learning process. The child is pulled out of their own intimate mindset and reckoning with challenges at hand and is thrust into the neurotic mental and emotional landscape of the parent. Children will set about trying to fix their parents or live the unlived life of the parents but this never works. Some people even succeed in fulfilling their parents' dreams but the rewards that come out of this are intrinsically tied to gaining the approval of the parents. A person can spend decades of their life in a process that is not self-generated. Most, so as to not have a lot of painful childhood memories surface, will then have a midlife crisis of some kind where they double down on unconsciously seeking their parents' approval by living their unlived dreams. The later a person goes into their life carrying the self-esteem wounds of their parents, the harder it is to undo the course things have taken. The cost for this is depression and the transmission of insecurities to the next generation.

9) Delivering edicts to the child

It is important that children obey their parents but parents must be morally upstanding so that they are authorities worth obeying. This is not some Herculean task. Peaceful parenting is a proactive approach that is easy to adopt and implement once the things parents do wrong and why are sufficiently illuminated. A parent who delivers edicts to a child learns quickly that simply telling the child what to do does not lead to further intimacy in the relationship. A cold distance forms over the years. Most parents assume this is simply natural. They cope with the distance by saying, "Teenagers will be teenagers!" or "Oh, she's just that way. She has her own mind about things." The truth is that people do not like being told what to do without understanding why they should do it. This author's hope for this book is that there is sufficient reasoning behind why some things are antithetical to good parenting and why some strategies are worth pursuing for the sake of good parenting.

Commandments even work, to a large degree, but the hostile elites draining the world of life right now prey upon the estrangement created between parent and child when commandments are simply handed down without rhyme or reason. The hostile elite overwhelm people in this condition with false choices, all of which lead to spiritual oblivion. Today's situation is like being told to eat meat and veggies your whole life without knowing exactly why you should and then some ringmaster leads you to an ice cream shop with seventy flavors of high fructose, soy garbage. "Doesn't that ice cream taste nummy?" asks the devilish ringmaster. "You see, you weren't allowed to taste all this sweetness!" Another analogy that comes to mind here is the story of Pinocchio being led astray by a pedophilic slave master to the Island of Pleasure where the boys turn into donkeys. The promise of easy answers beckons to the person who has not been taught how to reason through things.

Intimacy requires that we work thoroughly through the metaphysics of social, economic, and political problems with our children rather than give them a set of conclusions that looks good on paper and keeps civilization going if everyone just unflinchingly obeys. Not everyone is going to unflinchingly obey. Because of the deconstructive nature of Marxism, people have come to feel entitled to explore all those garbage flavors of ice cream. There is enough fiat and consumer credit pumping through the world that the illusion of deliverance from natural consequences has been temporarily achieved. People can stray from the traditional, Christian ethics without seeing immediate, harsh consequences such as there always was for the majority of human existence. Marxism gives excuses for people of low moral development to justify their failures. Marxism is an easy-out, for the time being, for parents to divorce themselves from the catastrophic parenting strategy of, "Well, she didn't do what I told her to do and now she ended up like so-and-so. Not my fault!" More on that in the neglect section coming up.

10) Overwhelming the child with pressure when the child does not understand what is going on

Patience is a virtue. Parents have their own schedules they must maintain in order to be profitable. Especially when a parent is an employee, their work schedules are dictated by someone else. This becomes especially problematic when the mother is not in the home. Maybe she gets better health insurance than the man. Maybe she out-earns him to a large degree. Maybe she is fast tracked for management. After all, what woman is *not* fast tracked for management in 2020? Or perhaps she has some work-from-home situation where she is around more often than if she were off in some giant building somewhere but still, she is firmly rooted to the home office. The time crunch is largely a result of whether the married parents have accepted or rejected the moral imperative to have the mother stay at home. Children need both parents around early in their development but they especially need maternal nurturance, the IQ bump that only a mother can provide through her consistent breastfeeding schedule[22], intimacy that bonds child to mother that comes from breastfeeding in person instead of bottle feeding when work allows, and the center of existential security in the home that roots the child for the rest of their life in a secure worldview. Parents who have

---

[22] https://www.theguardian.com/lifeandstyle/2015/mar/18/brazil-longer-babies-breastfed-more-achieve-in-life-major-study

the mother working, especially before the age of reason[23], have failed to emotionally mature in time to have a family. We, of course, must grant some allowances for the lunatic culture of feminism that has swept the world and the economic, *Women Who Work*[24] mantras of people such as Ivanka Trump having taken such deep root. These women will say, "Honor yourself by exploring the kind of life you deserve." This New Age mantra of free choice necessarily comes at the expense of young children, who naturally and categorically yearn for parental engagement *at least* every ten minutes of the day throughout their early development. While feminist careerists navel gaze at vision boards designed with the economic envies of geriatric financiers in mind, children remain unborn. Personal fulfillment for a woman has nothing to do with career and everything to do with spiritual development, role maturation as a mother and grandmother, and significant intimacy experiences with her children.

The woman is responsible for the time crunch experienced in the family, with respect to the children. Men are in charge of the entire family system and it is their work in the world that ultimately shelters the children from pressures the child is not prepared for. Men are made to work. They are at either ends of the bell curve of intelligence. Their musculature is more advanced across all races. Their naturally occurring hormonal profile gives them much higher risk tolerance. Their thinking is geared toward complexity and depth, as opposed to multi-tasking and socializing. Men can work long hours more easily than women can. Men deal with pressure better than women do.

The most perceptive children learn from what their parents do *under pressure* by figuring how they can work smarter. Good parents give

---

[23] https://www.scholastic.com/parents/family-life/social-emotional-learning/development-milestones/age-reason.html

[24] https://www.amazon.com/Women-Who-Work-Rewriting-Success/dp/0735211329

their children the lessons and insights necessary to work harder. Great parents help their children work smarter. When the child is of the age of reason, a father begins to teach the child the rudiments of his productive, profitable work in the world. This "fast forwards" the child in their productivity. Children are robbed of this intergenerational advantage when parents work highly technical, licensed managerial work that would not exist if it were not for the mountain of fiat in the economy and the African nihilism that has set into the culture since the advent of the welfare state and crummy mass migration. Parents are not all that motivated to "pass down" rat race, attend-dumb-meetings-all-day "skills". They are motivated to take the edge off their coffee addictions when they get home by plopping themselves down on the couch to watch techno-trash entertainment. Nobody comes home with the thought, "Today I am going to discuss with my kid how to retrain his foreign replacements one day." Nobody wants to teach their kid how to kiss ass with the tenured department head. Where the economy is junk, the parenting quality necessarily is impacted. Honest, productive enterprise puts totally different parenting incentives into the mix. Before the industrial revolution, parents lived where they worked and much of their skills necessarily were passed down or it meant starvation and poverty for the family. This kind of work still exists and much of it is coming back because white people are figuring out that hey, it is not all that appealing to commute two hours every day just to fart around in a cubicle in some giant tower nearby a Federal Reserve bank.

A lot of parents *do* pass down great things to their children and there will be ample acknowledgement of these achievements later on in the book.

Feminism destroys families and cripples their potential by not leveling about the relevant facts when it comes to female fertility. Women are most fertile from the legal age of consent in America, where this book is being written, to age 32.[25] The British Fertility Society writes:

> Women's fertility will continue to decrease every year, whether or not she is healthy and fit because the number and quality of the eggs decreases with age. Even if a woman is not ovulating (for example if she is taking the contraceptive pill, or is pregnant), the number of eggs continues to decline at the same rate. How quick a woman's fertility declines will depend on a combination of genetic and lifestyle (e.g. smoking) factors.

Feminism tells women that they should do what men do and enter the workforce at a young age, chase a career, be self-oriented about their bodies (instead of being family-oriented), that men should be doing housework, and that women are equal in their decision-making capacities to men. Feminism is an irredeemable label. Some boring women try to say that feminism is "akshually" traditionalism or they try to insert feminism into traditionalism and then hide it because that is part of their grift but the term is dead. The term is synonymous with evil and there are hundreds of millions of children aborted or unborn stacked up in a grisly pile of horror to prove so.

The best thing a woman can do is be a great mother. The second-best thing a woman can do is be an awesome grandmother. The third-best thing a woman can do is be a good aunt. This is because women consistently underperform against men in the workplace.[26] This is also because men cannot outperform women at being mothers but a man on his worst day will outperform a woman at being a father. This is also why it is so dangerous that "les-bee-YUN" (lesbian) couples are adopting and

---

[25] https://www.britishfertilitysociety.org.uk/fei/at-what-age-does-fertility-begin-to-decrease/

[26] https://www.prageru.com/video/there-is-no-gender-wage-gap/

having children. The workplace is for men. Fatherhood is for men. Everything else is a distortion based on Marxist lies about the nature of men and women.

Men have no need to do housework. They need to go out and engage in moral, productive exchange. The research points away from housework for men:

> Conventional wisdom suggests that women are drawn to men who help out around the house. Yet new research indicates that some divisions of labor may be sexier than others. A February paper in the American Sociological Review reported that married couples in which men take on a greater share of the dishes, laundry and other traditionally female chores had sex less often than average, which in this study was about five times a month. Yet couples in which men confined themselves largely to traditionally male chores such as yard work enjoyed sex more frequently than average. Taken to the extreme, men who performed all the traditionally female chores would have had sex 1.6 times less often than men who did none of them.[27]

While women with low sex drives, toxic careerism in their minds, and adrenal fatigue from coffee addictions in their bodies may not value the loss of sex in a marriage (and thus fewer children), women who clean up from feminism commonly have massive, unrepairable regrets from the years lost living for something other than fertility and spiritual development.[28]

---

[27] https://www.scientificamerican.com/article/men-who-do-housework-have-less-sex/

[28] https://www.thecatholicthing.org/2018/07/11/the-bitter-truth-about-feminism/

Nor are women equally capable in their ability to manage financial decisions, compared to men. The top 30 richest people in the world list only features women because the women either stole the money from their ex-husbands through the wacko divorce laws on the books today in America or because they inherited from a great patriarch.[29] Women are disproportionately affected by divorce because they do not have the earning power that men do:

For women approaching or in retirement, becoming divorced, widowed or unemployed had detrimental effects on their income security. Moreover, divorce and widowhood had more pronounced effects for women than for men. For example, women's household income, on average, fell by 41 percent with divorce, almost twice the size of the decline that men experienced. For widowhood, women's household income fell by 37 percent—while men's declined by only 22 percent. Unemployment also had a detrimental effect on income security, though the effects were similar for women and men; household assets and income fell by 7 to 9 percent.[30]

The data reveals that women earn less than men, only count in the super wealthy because of inheritance or divorce, and are by and large crushed by the economic outcomes of divorce. Yet feminism gins women up to encroach into the realm of men, gossip with other feminist women about the shortcomings of men, and to be autonomous economic units so that they can spend their money on consumer goods and look fashionable for other women. Since women in a feminist order do not have to face the prospect of using their 20's for childrearing, their personalities do not experience the natural pressures to be charming, agreeable, and sweet. Take famous feminist Ivanka Trump, for example. The supplicant aspect of her personality is deliberately there to impress foreign investors, cheap

---

[29] https://www.forbes.com/billionaires/

[30] https://www.gao.gov/assets/600/592727.pdf

labor bosses, Chinese banksters, and Islamic heads of state, not Middle American captains of industry. She could not be bothered to visit West Virginia or Idaho except to get tasteful family photos for magazine photo shoots. Contrast her against Melania Trump, who was raised in a traditional society. The supplicant aspect of her personality serves to guide her son, Barron, into the executive position Donald Trump currently serves in and to love the American people as a pious mother. The results could not be more contrasted. Of the two, Melania, as a representative of traditional feminine virtues, offers a more enjoyable and long-term, stable marriage prospect for a man over Ivanka Trump. Melania will age with wisdom whereas Ivanka's spiritual nature is that of a self-conscious addict who makes her parenting into a kind of marketing exhibition to cleanse her conscience of her careerist guilt. Feminism roots ambition into the feminine psyche whereas our pre-central banking, Christian order selected *against* ambition in women. Ambitious women only ever served as a cautionary tale of what *not* to do. Ambitious women have always contributed to the rack and ruin of civilization.

Men and women who learn to rely on each other for their naturally-occurring, God-given strengths come to an intimate involvement and strength of love that modern feminism (and whatever contrived variant some quirky woman out there invents) cannot offer. The best income security for a woman is to adhere to a value-creating man, make him nutritious meals, support his sleep by keeping a lovely home, and to bear him and homeschool him sons that will take on his work as he ages. Governments across the West are already running out of money. They have busied themselves with dumping obscene amounts of currency to prop up favored sectors of the economy so as to stave off ruin and revolution.[31] We cannot continue to propagate the lie that women should burn up their fertility windows giving PowerPoint presentations,

---

[31] https://www.bloomberg.com/news/articles/2020-09-03/macron-throws-100-billion-euros-at-french-economic-relaunch

accumulating tiny apartment dogs, dating around like whores (emphasis New Yorker accent), and building up emotional grudges against men when inevitably they cannot measure up. Hiring managers still prefer to hire men and the reason is not difficult to explain:

> A recent study, published by Proceedings of the National Academy of Sciences, finds that managers of both sexes are twice as likely to hire a man as a woman.
>
> The study, conducted by business-school professors from Columbia University, Northwestern University, and the University of Chicago, asked male and female managers to recruit people to handle simple mathematical tasks. The applicants had equal skills, but managers of both genders were more likely to hire men.
>
> The male candidates boasted about their abilities, while women downplayed their talents, but the managers didn't compensate for the difference when making hiring decisions. When the managers were explicitly shown the women could perform the tasks just as well as the men, the result was still that men were 1.5 times more likely to be hired. Even worse, when managers hired a job applicant who performed worse on the test than a fellow candidate, two-thirds of the time the lesser candidate was a man.[32]

Ivy League educated female journalists have been straining themselves trying to do mental backflips so that hiring managers will hire women at a higher rate. They write books with insecure titles like *We Demand To Be Taken Seriously* or *Women Are The Best At Business*. They start gender consulting firms that roam the corporate landscape looking for a man to

---

[32] https://www.inc.com/will-yakowicz/how-to-help-end-gender-bias-while-hiring.html

isolate and then kick in the testicles for profit. No matter what they do, these hardcore feminists cannot explain away the basic facts: women are more expensive to hire because they take maternity leave, disrupt training and teambuilding processes when they leave for maternity leave, and take tremendous resources to retrain when they reenter the work force later in life. Businesses do not want to absorb those costs. Corporations are one Democrat President away from openly discouraging women from reproducing.

Feminism's answer is to nudge women toward not having children at all. Women develop depression when they do not have children, as they are denying their life's basic purpose, and go on psychiatric medications in middle age. Women 45 years old and older have the highest usage of psychiatric medications of all age groups between men and women. Psychiatric medication use is up across the board:

> More than a quarter of American women (26%) take such drugs -- including antidepressants, anti-anxiolytics, attention deficit-hyperactivity disorder (ADHD) drugs, and atypical antipsychotics. That compares with 15% of men.

> Of the four classes, antidepressants were the most commonly used drug. Just over 20% of women older than 20 took antidepressants, and that proportion jumped 29% between 2001 and 2010, according to the report.

> Older women -- those 65 and up -- accounted for the largest proportion of the increase, the researchers wrote, and while men use antidepressants far less, the number of antidepressant prescriptions for them was up 29% over 10 years.

Women need a stable and secure domestic existence where they can tend to children and then grandchildren peaceably. The workplace, despite the fluorescent lighting and air conditioning, is still a harsh place unsuited for the social needs (which are great) of women. Women should not be pumping themselves full of wine, antidepressants, inhaled dog fur particles, and coffee. It just so turns out that men's sperm is exactly what middle-aged women need:

> Vaginal tissue is very absorptive. It's richly endowed with blood and lymph vessels. Given vaginal absorptiveness and all the mood-elevating compounds found in semen, Gallup, Burch, and SUNY colleague Steven Platek wondered if semen exposure might be associated with better mood and less depression. They surveyed 293 college women at SUNY Albany about intercourse with and without condoms and then gave the women the Beck Depression Inventory, a standard test of mood. Compared with women who "always" or "usually" used condoms, those who "never" did, whose vaginas were exposed to semen, showed significantly better mood—fewer depressive symptoms, and fewer bouts of depression. In addition, compared to women who had no intercourse at all, the semen-exposed women showed more elevated mood and less depression.[33]

Risky sex is associated with depression but middle-aged women who are married can have all the unprotected sex they want, especially after menopause, but whether they *should* is yet another question. A stable marriage and children in the home save women from listless lives of loneliness, cats, psychiatry, and bitter liberal politics in their 40's. The husband puts literal natural anti-depressants into the woman and enlists in her the noble cause of the next generation's upbringing. When a woman is in an improved mood, she is less likely to put stress on her children, less likely to misallocate her time resources into pursuits that

[33] https://www.psychologytoday.com/us/blog/all-about-sex/201101/attention-ladies-semen-is-antidepressant

hamper quality family time, and more likely to take an agreeable stance with her husband.

Aside from family structure considerations and a takedown of feminism, parents, as a behavioral event, also overwhelm their children with pressure when the child does not understand what is going on. The scenario is as follows. A child finds his way into the bottles of pills under the bathroom sink. He is playing with the lids and finding he can pour the pills out onto the floor. The boy decides to sample the pills and puts one in his mouth. All of this happens in the span of thirty seconds. The mother returns from her trip to the garbage can or putting away a broom and dustpan or whatever. She is frightened that the boy will choke or get horribly sick from something his developing system cannot process. She howls at the boy to stop, to not put the pills in his mouth. Maybe she has told him this before. She chides him for knowing he should not put pills in his mouth yet continuing to do it.

This is a mild event and it has happened pre-memory for the boy. The howling component is *usually* unnecessary and puts the child into a fear state. The chiding or the reminding is dysfunctional because children take time to learn some things. Just ask any mother who has had to potty train for longer than a couple months. Another point of consideration is how the mother looms large over the toddler boy. This is into the sensitive stuff now but it is worth mentioning. Children experience their parents as giants, metaphorically and literally. Why are pills at floor level? Why is there not a child lock on the cabinet? Why is the parent even taking all those pills?! Could the parent do without them with a bit of self-reflection? If there is parental failure on any of these questions, why does a literal human giant need to be enforcing a pill aversion after the fact? We do not want our children putting things from off the floor or from non-food containers into their bodies, granted. Why the theatricality, though? If your kid takes a hard tumble or puts pills in their mouths, with self-knowledge it eventually takes only a moment for you to acknowledge your own fear so that you can gently and assertively handle the situation. Some parents are looking for dramas and so a hard spill or dog poop in the mouth becomes this *loud* thing put into the face of the toddler or child. Kids have no need for this. These grand shows serve to overwhelm the kid, make the kid avoidant of sensation seeking (which is vital for childhood learning), and if the production is grand enough, start to twist the kid into a "freeze" stance when they are a natural fight or flight type. Worse yet is when a second parent joins in the fray. Two literal human giants exasperatingly asking a kid over and over why the kid was told not to do x, y, or z and yet the kid keeps doing it. Kids are in-process. They enjoy making mistakes. They are not mistake averse like neurotic parents are. Kids like testing their parents. This is not cause for melodrama. Simple, calm corrections that bring the child and the parent closer are all that is required. Anything beyond this is detrimental to the child, even if it is a mild event.

Shaming is another behavior that bears mentioning in this section on the mistakes parents make. To shame a child is to *make personal* the mistakes of a child. Children make mistakes every single day. A parent shames a child by communicating there is something wrong or defective about the child for the mistakes they make. Shaming a child is a form of resentment from the parent, a dysfunctional disposition that develops over time. The fundamental component of shame that differentiates it from common disapproval is that the parent is putting on to the child their own uncomfortable feelings that the child cannot process. For example, a disapproving look when a child is about to push their sibling over or go down a slide the wrong way is not shaming, per se. The added dimension to make it shaming would be an overemphasis in the look to put fear, a self-disgust response (shame), or sadness into the child. Shame is completely foreign to innocent children. It is the parent who introduces this to the child's life. Children learn *humility* as part of their natural learning and growing process. They test limits in the world and recalibrate their expectations and play accordingly. A parent is who properly emotionally calibrated, that is to say that they are competent peaceful parents, does not artificially narrow the horizons of a child – thus giving the child a neurotic sense of limits.

Shaming provokes all manner of dysfunction in the child. Krystine I. Batcho Ph.D. from Psychology Today writes:

> Achieving change or elimination of certain overt behaviors can have its own inherent value. For example, eliminating child abuse by shaming abusers would enhance the lives of children spared abuse. However, if a person is so highly motivated to engage in a behavior or believes they are not able to inhibit it, shame might result in efforts to hide the unacceptable behaviors—effectively driving the perpetrator to secrecy, deception, and even threatening victims to silent them—all in an effort to escape detection. If fueled by anxiety, victimless habits such as overeating, cutting, or bulimia could increase as the shamed individual self-isolates to avoid public censure or attempts at intervention. Driving someone 'underground' can be counterproductive.[34]

People who were shamed often in childhood are unable in adulthood to process feelings of frustration, disappointment, and anger in the people around them as adults. A person who was crushed in childhood by shaming from their parents perceives in adulthood that others are commonly unfair with them and walks through life as a perpetual victim. This person pushes away those who can see through the toxic shame to the *real* person inside them. The tragedy of a person crushed in childhood

---

[34] https://www.psychologytoday.com/us/blog/longing-nostalgia/201705/why-shaming-doesnt-work

by shame is years and even decades of difficulties in having good boundaries and regulating a steady sense of self in adulthood.

Shaming perpetrators out in the world or a kid who is physically attacking your kid at the park, or something like this, may be necessary out of third-party self-defense but that is more outside the scope of this book. The madness of worldwide Communism is that because of its inversion of values, people are forced to reckon with its agents in a manner outside of reason. Peaceful parenting is to reason through all difficulties with a child. Some people would say, "Well, Mr. Franssen, fat shaming is statistically proven to work." It may work between adults as obesity, before the Industrial Revolution, was always seen as an attack on the tribe and an unnecessary and immoral draw on the tribe or village's resources. Fat shaming has no place in parenting. Simply not feeding your kid sugar, giving them food to manage your uncomfortable internal states or to soothe them, and dumping processed foods from your diet is good enough. These are easy adjustments. Fat shaming between adults is far after the fact.

Adults who shame children feel ashamed themselves. There is no good reason under the sun to shame your own child. Some children cry more than others. Some children have more sleep troubles than others. Some children learn to read later than others. The list goes on and on. This is not a reason to begin to feel you have failed somehow and then to overcompensate for that feeling by putting something noxious into your child's psyche that was not there before. Life is messy. Shame demands that life be tidy and trouble free. Shame breeds fragility and emotional distance between a parent and child. There is no need for this. Kids do not need to hide from peaceful parents but if they do, for whatever reason, this is not occasion to introduce dissociation to the relationship. Shame is not argument!

The third, and worst, category of abuse that parents engage in is neglect. Neglect is the worst, in most cases, because it is the *absence* of parenting. As macabre as it sounds, a child reckons that at least she is getting touch, attention, and some trouble to work through when she is spanked compared to a grey void of nothing. According to the US Children's Bureau, neglect is the most common form of child abuse:

As in previous years, neglect was overwhelmingly the most common form of child maltreatment.

CPS investigations determined the following:

-60.8 percent of victims suffered neglect.

-10.7 percent of victims suffered physical abuse.

-7.0 percent of victims suffered sexual abuse.

-2.3 percent of victims suffered psychological maltreatment.

-0.8 percent of victims suffered medical neglect.

-2.7 percent of victims experienced "other" maltreatment, which may include threatened abuse or parental substance use. States define "other" differently, but it generally refers to any maltreatment that does not fit in one of the NCANDS categories.[35]

Neglect is convenient to bad parents because it is the absence of effort. Children provide an unending myriad of challenges on a daily basis to the parent. Some parents just want to give up. People who give up on parenting "in defeat" have not dealt with their feelings of low self-worth, often coming from having been defeated by their own parents in

---

[35] https://www.childwelfare.gov/pubPDFs/canstats.pdf

childhood. These people gave up on their dreams somewhere along the way and so they have a deadened inner life that leaves them apathetic about the dreams of their children.

For this discussion of neglect, we need to cover the types of neglect. In a bit I will also cover two types of neglect that do no receive as much mention as forms of neglect. The types of neglect, according to Kaplan, are:

Physical Neglect or Deprivation of Needs Neglect

This type of neglect occurs when children's basic physical needs (e.g., food, shelter, and clothing) are not being met and often occurs in a persistent pattern. Examples of physical deprivation include being denied food and/or water and being left out in the elements. (*Author's note: This type of neglect is more common in developing nations. America continues to have a strong culture around keeping children clothed and fed, although childhood obesity rates are high among non-whites.[36] Poor hygiene is also a form of physical neglect. Victims of this kind of abuse suffer from dental problems, head lice, head wounds from a lack of washing and brushing, and even things like being the 'stinky kid' in school.*)

Medical Neglect

When medical neglect occurs, children are denied the medical care they need to treat a condition or prevent an illness from worsening. A child may be repeatedly refused medical care for an ongoing condition or may only be denied for a one-time instance of required medical care. Failing to secure medical attention for an injured child or withholding care with the intent to cause death are both examples of medical neglect. (*One manner in*

---

[36] https://www.cdc.gov/obesity/data/childhood.html

which medical neglect is commonly observed, thanks to rabid coverage by the mainstream media, is via 'alternative healing' schemes. Western medicine has its obvious, massive problems but it is important to remember that these are largely the result of mega-government largesse. Medicine was making leaps and bounds in progress prior to Lyndon Johnson's Great Society welfare reforms.)

Supervisory Neglect

Supervisory neglect occurs when the adult responsible for a child either fails to supervise and keep the child from being harmed or fails to have someone else supervise the child and keep him or her from harm. This type of neglect can occur continually or only happen one time. Two examples of supervisory neglect include failing to supervise a child around weapons and other dangerous circumstances and leaving a child with an impaired caregiver. (*Unintentional drowning in the United States averages about ten deaths a day. Nonfatal drowning injuries can cause severe brain damage, resulting in long-term disabilities such as memory problems and permanent loss of basic functioning.[37] Leaving your child unattended near or in water is never worth the few moments you think you are saving in taking care of other stuff.*

Another huge and common failure in the supervisory role of a parent is sleep schedule neglect. A staggering 57.8% of middle school students and 72.7% of high school students in the United States are not getting enough sleep on school nights.[38] Children

---

[37] https://www.cdc.gov/homeandrecreationalsafety/water-safety/waterinjuries-factsheet.html
[38] https://www.cdc.gov/features/students-sleep/index.html

with sleep disturbances develop into adults with sleep disturbances. Good sleep is a marker of mental well-being and the backbone of the day's mood, productivity, creativity, and social opportunities. Parents who fail to inculcate their children with a consistent, adequate sleep schedule are generally themselves up late with electronic devices, unable to manage their moods, eating late into the night, and neglectful of the responsibilities associated with creating a physical environment in the bedroom conducive to a good night's sleep. "Fighting against sleep" is a common symptom of emotional trauma. So is the late hour consumption of caffeine.)

Environmental Neglect

The fourth type of neglect is related to both physical neglect and supervisory neglect, but it occurs when children's home environments are filthy. Rotting food may be left out, there may be infestations of rats or cockroaches, and children may regularly come to school in dirty clothing. Some professionals group environmental neglect with physical neglect. (*According to the CDC, dust mites, pet fur, mold and cockroach droppings left unclean trigger asthma attacks in children.*[39] *People who had filthy homes as children struggle to find housework fulfilling as adults.*)

Educational Neglect

Educational neglect is when children are not given access to education. Examples of educational neglect include parents failing to register children for school or parents making children stay home from school to ensure that they don't report the abuse they experience at home. (*Failing to register children for school is*

---

[39] https://howtoadult.com/consequences-children-filthy-homes-8202594.html

obviously not a form of educational neglect, to the degree that public schools have become indoctrination camps and considering whether or not the parent is educating the child in the home. You have no moral obligation to register your children with the state in any form. Doing so is at your individual discretion and a consideration of what advantages are proffered or bureaucratic time-wasting you will save your child in the future. Public education is not a human right and public school teachers are not essential workers, though education in some form certainly is essential for children. A good place to start is self-knowledge. My self-knowledge lecture series The Road To Self-Knowledge is available through my website StevenFranssen.com. I will also be writing homeschool curriculum in the years to come so keep an eye out!)

Emotional Neglect

Emotional neglect occurs when children are deprived of their emotional needs (forming secure, positive attachments with adults). Some researchers group emotional neglect with other types of neglect. Parents may struggle to meet children's emotional needs due to a variety of reasons, such as depression or drug and alcohol abuse. A few examples of emotional neglect include humiliating a child, rejecting a child, or giving bizarre forms of punishment.[40] *(One common form of emotional neglect is stonewalling. A person who stonewalls another person does so by disengaging unfairly and refusing to engage in discussion, problem-solving, or cooperation. They usually sit silently and sullenly in order to provoke feelings of abandonment in the other party. This is an effective, though cruel, method of forcing compliance out of a child – especially one who is not confident.*

---

[40] https://www.kaplanco.com/ii/six-types-of-neglect

*Confident children do not respond to stonewalling as they have
rich inner lives and simply concern themselves with other pursuits.*

*Confident children do not speak the 'language of abuse' as they are
capable of meeting their own needs to a large degree and simply do
not click into place with the psychodramas of immature adults.)*

Abandonment is stonewalling taken to its extreme. Parents who abandon
their children do so quite literally by dumping their children off at
government buildings (public schooling is a not insignificant form of
abandonment) or by leaving their child with family members. The parent
can abandon their child to a grandparent and live and work a town away
but remember, children do not have accurate gauges of distance. Until
they are well into the age of reason and can begin to understand
geography and the implications of travel, any distance away from their
primary caretaker is magnified well beyond an adult's understanding of
distance.

When a child is an infant, waking up from a nap is troubling
because mother has *disappeared*. Abandonment is the renunciation of
responsibility of a child in all forms and in particular, it is an emotional
withdrawal. Some people need childcare or help from extended family.
This is not abandonment. But "loving" a child from a distance while
doing stuff like watching too much TV or whoring around in Las Vegas
does count as abandonment. The complex scenarios of yesteryear wherein
there was the semblance of justification for parent-child separation are
gone. Now there are divorce courts and they rip families apart, usually in
favor of the mother against the father. Feminism has become legally
weaponized. Fathers who are torn from their children by witchy judges
and law-bound cops are not abandoners. Good fathers indeed fight hard
to keep their children from the predations of the family courts such as
Michael, from Frisco, Texas, who with his lawyer saved his daughter from

sexual abuse she was experiencing at the hands of her mother's fiancé.[41]
These heartwarming stories are the exception but they *are* shining
examples of First World parenting.

Abandonment is tragic for children because children do not have
a choice whether they come into the world or not. Their parents made
that choice for them. Parenting is not an at-will arrangement. People
make the choice to become parents when they engage in the sex act with a
member of the opposite sex. Birth control failure rates are commonly
below 1%[42] but the very notion of birth control is a liberal attack on the
family unit. Children who are parented well come into adulthood
prepared to be parents, even at the tender age of 18. Birth control
undermines traditional family values, extended familial and religious
networks, and the love bond between husband and wife. Sex is not for
pleasure. Sex is for procreation. People who use sex for pleasure alone
become perverted. Women become feminists. Men become simps[43].
Pregnancy, childbirth, and parenting are the natural buttresses against the
unbridled destructive force of recreational sex. Birth control is the foreign
substance or object inserted into the body by government subsidized
organizations (and people who have received indoctrination from the
government and media) so that young, fertile people can join in the
crazed orgy destroying Western Civilization. People who handwave off
the destructiveness of sex for pleasure are people who cannot accurately
track hidden costs. Super massive social, cultural, and financial subsidies
exist in modern society to obscure the familial costs of welfare. These
same hand-wavers usually are one of two siblings or have had more than
one partner or have never known or married a childhood sweetheart.

---

[41] https://www.dailymail.co.uk/news/article-8715845/Father-WINS-
custody-9-year-old-daughter-sparked-StandWithSophie-campaign.html
[42] https://www.cdc.gov/reproductivehealth/contraception/index.htm
[43] A man who foolishly overvalues and defers to a woman, putting her on a
pedestal.

Cynicism and "it's fine!" are not arguments. They will say, "Having sex for pleasure *once* will not kill you." This completely misses the point. We have to think of the compounding effects of *everyone* having this attitude versus if everyone had a "sex for procreation" attitude. The results speak for themselves. Sex can be for connection but only between a married man and woman. Any other way and it is a form of dissociation between the parties involved. Back to abandonment: because children did not choose to come into the world, they cannot be held morally accountable for whatever justifications the parent has in mind for abandoning the child. If children could advocate successfully for themselves in the face of child abuse, they would say something along the lines of, "Wait, it was *you* who brought me into this world. You are going to bring me into this world and then abuse me? I didn't deserve any of this!" Indeed, children do not deserve an ounce of abuse no matter how "naughty" their parents raised them to be.

The Boomer and Generation X generations are guilty of a liberal parenting style that can best be described as "libertarian renouncement". The line follows, "You're an adult now. You're gonna do what you're going to do. We did the best we could." The effect of this parenting has been to leave Millennials and Gen Z to the wolves only the wolves are: pornography, a moon crater of a job landscape, virulent Marxism in the universities, and hyper wealthy pedophiles who express their anxieties through mega corporations. While it is true that when people become moral agents as biological adults, they are responsible for their own decisions, it is not like we can turn a blind eye to the previous 18 years of neglect and inability to convey to their children the relevant facts on the part of Boomer and Gen X parents. There is a delicate balance here to walk because Boomer and Gen X'ers were plopped in front of TVs and told to go to college, where marijuana and the sexual revolution were available in massive doses. Furthermore, no one was all that inoculated against CIA television programming in the 50's through the 21st century.

It is only in the past fifteen years, and basically into the Wild West days of social media which ended in about 2017, that masses of people have been waking up to their own emotional estrangement from their families and how this was stoked by hostile elites on the Coasts. This situation is being remediated in a thousand different ways but the prevailing theme is admission of guilt on the part of the older generation which is counterbalanced by a commitment of the younger generations to the revival of traditional social values. The family institution is being reenergized by conservatives who are becoming ever more conservative since the age of the Internet.[44] Our best and brightest young people are leading everyone back to a good place.

Divorce

Divorce destroys families. Divorce is an admission of failure. The parents failed to properly vet one another before marriage. The parents failed to align themselves on first principles and values before having children. The parents failed to keep one another honest by practicing moral courage and emotional vulnerability during their time together. One or both parents failed to resolve their addictions in a timely manner. One or both parents succumbed to external forces outside the family that preyed upon their internal weaknesses. Divorce, in its modern institutional form, is commonly attributable to feminism, the rise of secularism, government largesse, and Internet pornography. Studies have found that roughly 60% of divorces have reported that Internet pornography played a significant role in the divorces.[45] Pornography erodes the love bond between parents because the porn user develops a false bond to the performers on screen. The porn user idealizes their love needs into the performers and slips into

---

[44] https://www.pewresearch.org/politics/2014/06/12/political-polarization-in-the-american-public/

[45] https://verilymag.com/2017/07/causes-of-divorce-effects-of-watching-pornography

a world of fantasy where, through sexual stimulation, the user can be saved from his or her problems- however momentarily. Porn users begin to look outside the marriage in the real world:

> Scholars were quick to point out the potential for pornography to alter "sexual scripts"—our expectations for how sexual activity (and romantic relationships generally) should proceed (Berger, Simon, & Gagnon, 1973)—and inform relationship norms (e.g., how often oral sex should occur) and characteristics (e.g., fidelity). This influence was first presented in a positive light, with pornography ostensibly creating more effective sexual scripts (Berger et al., 1973). It is possible, however, because pornography generally portrays uncommitted—and often explicitly unfaithful—sexual encounters, that exposure can foster a permissive sexual script, increasing acceptance of extradyadic behavior (Braithwaite, Coulson, Keddington, & Fincham, 2014).

The available data are in strong support of the assertion that individuals exposed to larger amounts of nonviolent pornography evidence an increased acceptance and estimated frequency of extramarital sex (Zillmann & Bryant, 1988a) relative to controls and are more likely to believe that promiscuity is natural and that marriage is less desirable. Also, males who watched a pornographic movie within the previous year were more likely to be accepting of extramarital sex, had an increased number of sexual partners within the past year, and were more likely to engage in paid sex behavior than those who did not (Wright & Randall, 2012). Pornography consumption also predicted casual sex behavior (including extramarital sex)

3 years later, with no evidence of reverse causality (Wright, 2012).[46]

Pornography normalizes every sexual deviancy under the sun. Users experience chemical rewards for using it. The chemical reward rewires daily behavior and softens attitudes about infidelity. Users bond to "virtual girlfriends" or boyfriends, an infidelity itself. Marital dissatisfaction increases, conflicts form, and the marriage heads down the rocky slopes toward divorce.

The common trope of divorce being brought on by alcoholism and spousal battery has given way to a whole host of ideological maladies eroding the bond between man and woman. Of course, a battered woman needs to get away from her husband. Of course, a cheating wife should be served divorce papers. Of course, there are sensible reasons why people must separate but these are reasons that come after the fact of intimacy and responsibility failure. This is why people should marry first and foremost for values and personal excellence, and then secondarily for looks, money, convenience, lust, sex, business, or for the sake of others in the community. Marriage, as an institution in the West and prior to the welfare state, was successful because people were encouraged to marry according to the Christian tradition: by their moral conscience. This had an uplifting, IQ-increasing effect on the population. The West has always granted more freedom to women in matters of marriage. Marxism has preyed upon this fact by using the welfare state to make men and women resentful of one another in order to provoke an overreaction (instead of a return to historical norms) that will justify more state intervention. The solution to systemic divorce is peaceful parenting and a commitment to

---

[46] https://www.yourbrainonporn.com/relevant-research-and-articles-about-the-studies/porn-use-sex-addiction-studies/a-historical-and-empirical-review-of-pornography-and-romantic-relationships-implications-for-family-researchers-2015/

moral excellence in partner selection. Recreational sex clouds people's judgement, as does pre-marital sex. Both of these are far common than moral excellence in partner selection. Do the math. This is not a winning situation. We have to turn it around.

Divorce ravages children. Divorce is a split between the mother and father principle in the child's concept formation. The child is denied the clarity of thinking that results from emotional balance in the home. Now the child must contend with the fallout of the divorce. The child must be at odds with oneself because the parts of the mother and parts of the father in the child's psyche have reached an irreconcilable end. Parents further exacerbate the damage by fighting and making a further spectacle of the divorce. Parents try to turn the child against the other parent. Strange men starting coming around the woman's domicile. These men are often sexual predators, spurred on by the momentum of being attracted to single moms. When a man does not have a biological investment in the child, it is easier for him to justify sexualizing the child of the single mom in addition to the mom herself. Lawyers come into the fold. Debts pile up. Parents scream at one another and have visitation stand-offs in parking lots. Each parent feels abandoned and doubles down on their emotional defenses. The child is thrust into this tornado of misery and agony. Children of divorce learn to shut down major components of their emotional lives in order to continue onward. They develop distractions and abstractions that offer them safety from the primordial psychic death struggle playing out in the family. Both parents are locked in, both trampling their emotional credibility in order to triumph over the other as "the parent who was less at fault." The divorce courts reward this at every turn. The truth gets lost in the shuffle. The child loses the harmonious presence of two parents at his side, looking over him benevolently. One or both parents gets lost in their own traumas. Eventually the dust settles. Sometimes years have passed. Nothing was resolved. People learned to live apart, that is all. The promise of true love slips from the child's grasp as the gods in his universe have mortally wounded one another. Nobody has the emotional mastery to nurture the child back to life. The child staggers into adulthood. According to a brand-new study from Baylor University:

> …researchers saw that the oxytocin levels in those who experienced parental divorce at a young age were much lower than the other participants'. They also found that these individuals rated their parents as 'less caring', their childhood selves as 'less confident' and 'less secure in relationships', and their current caregiving style as 'less sensitive' than the control group in the questionnaire portion.[47]

It is no secret that people whose parents divorce are at a much higher risk of divorcing and that children of divorce more often marry other children of divorce.[48] The catastrophic mental effects of divorce described in these pages, carry on for a lifetime. Parental separation, before the plentiful time of the Industrial Revolution, generally meant extreme hardship and the reasonable estimate that a sibling or two would die. Paternal abandonment, which modern divorce too often mimics, was a sure death sentence. There is hope for the next generation, however. Peaceful parenting can save couples from divorce.

---

[47] https://thriveworks.com/blog/levels-of-oxytocin-significantly-lower-in-adults-who-were-children-when-parents-divorced/

[48] https://www.wf-lawyers.com/divorce-statistics-and-facts/

Chapter Four: Laying The Foundations

Now that we have thoroughly established what peaceful parenting is *not*, we need to undertake the foundations for peaceful parenting. Philosophy offers us the tools to reflect on our prior experiences, the values we gained or were burdened with from these experiences, and the ability to reassess ourselves as our knowledge improves. As Socrates said, "It is better to change an opinion than to persist in a wrong one." Bringing the light of philosophy to our personal histories is difficult because our idealizations of our parents are tested. Some of them are undone. When we look at how our own parents did, through a moral lens, relationships can be put the test and painful, difficult conversations are broached where our sense of normalcy can be thrown out of balance.

Self-Knowledge

I have written an extensive discussion and primer on the fundamentals of self-knowledge in my book, *Make Self-Knowledge Great Again.*[49] The book offers extensive insights on the self-reflection process, tools for self-

---

[49] https://www.amazon.com/Make-Self-Knowledge-Great-Again-Principles-ebook/dp/B06WWRVG7P

therapy and trauma resolution, and principles for moral, adult living. For the purposes of this book, we will revisit self-knowledge and how it relates to peaceful parenting and then we will move on to the fundamentals of healthy marriage as they serve the purpose of parenting well.

The basic violation of peaceful parenting, of the child's personhood, is the imposition of the parent on the child the parent's unwanted, intolerable, uncomfortable, and unprocessed emotional states. Parents need self-knowledge so that they know what their tendencies as a parent will be. This knowledge can be had by a systematic exploration of one's own childhood memories, if possible, interviews with one's own parents, and the endeavor to heal traumas sufficiently so that one is not disrupting their children's development but instead working to foster the child's development at every turn.

This process begins with the question, "Who am I?" Everyone has an identity. Most people's identities are formed by the media and that is why we have a Marxist revolution underway in the West. People drunk on the media believe they are a dash of freedom fighter, somewhat hippy, drug and homosexuality accepting, consumeristic, compassionate empaths who are going to usher in a post-national order by shopping at Trader Joe's and worshipping athletes. People who are drunk on the media were left vulnerable to the media by the parenting they received. Their parents did not inoculate them against its predations. So, going a step deeper, we look at the identity formed in people by the common parenting doled out in the past two generations. The common liberal values passed on in parenting present themselves later in life as such:

My parents were okay. I dunno. I don't really think about it much.

Quality of parenting is not a concept commonly discussed with children. Children of abusive parents sometimes, of their own accord, become aware of "other options" when they spend time with less abused children. Since children are seen as possessions of their parents, akin to little slaves in the least developed places of the West, quality assurance is not brought to the table in the relational dynamics of the family. People do not conceive that there is a considerable upside to explaining the essential "contract" of parenting to a child: if I do a great job with you, our relationship when you are an adult will be an at-will, value-added one instead of a draining obligation. Liberal children are further pushed out of the franchise because old age care for their parents is an obligation everyone assumes the state will take on. Intergenerational integrity results when the foundational contractual nature of parenting is explained to the child. "Here is what I am doing. You can do this, too. It will serve us well, all of us together." Liberal parents leave their children in the Dark Ages of mental serfdom and menial slavery.

They wanted me to have an education so here I am in the city, getting a degree. They will be proud of me.

People have been raised to associate education with intelligence and wisdom. People want to be seen as competent in their chosen endeavors. Feminism tells women to chase careers, at extreme personal cost. Liberals see themselves as an enlightened elite prepared to take the reigns of the Therapeutic State. Who they are is wrapped up in a perfectionistic, over-socialized and invasive concern with the personal affairs of others. Liberal parenting is fundamentally out of control because it has no moral center. Victims of this parenting develop this chaos in their identities, to be held at bay by therapeutic techniques.

Yeah, I'm lonely every day but I try not to think about it. I distract myself instead!

Since educational attainment is highly prized in liberal homes, young people go out into the world to live in tiny apartments and go into debt getting degrees for jobs that no longer exist. This is a lonely prospect.

Liberal parenting does not empower children to identify as self-reflective people. It teaches children to double down when they are wrong, just as their parents double down on evil when dissident information makes it to their ears. Liberals chalk truths about the world up to "conspiracy theories" so as to keep their heads buried in the sand. Their children learn this from them.

My parents didn't tell me what's bad or good. Mostly they didn't talk to me about stuff.

Liberal parents do not teach their kids about systems of ethics or first principles because it would empower their kids to start to take into account the parenting process with a critical eye. Children are "deplatformed" by liberal parents through ignorance, through liberal shaming, or through indoctrination into a set of beliefs that places value on chaos and "the feelies" so that nothing essential is ever accomplished. When there is good and bad as considerations, liberal parenting posits empathy, compassion, and Science as the good and "the patriarchy" as bad. None of this means anything because science is now politicized and "the patriarchy" is a Marxist invention. "Empathy and compassion" in liberal circles simply means to be in an agreeable mood around others and to self-attack with ideological doubt if negative feelings arise. The liberal worldview is incoherent. It is a mental ghetto that serves international bankers. Since liberal adult-children have a need to idealize and protect their parents, they take on their parents' easy answers to moral questions as their own. "There's a terse man. He needs to be nice or he is evil! Good people smile. Bad people frown."

My parents let me experiment and that's groovy.

As stated earlier, liberal or libertarian parenting is all about renouncement of responsibility in these little rituals at different points of a child's development. Children are not discouraged from gender-inappropriate play because, "Openness, man!" Children are propagandized with, "Jimi Hendrix, man!" at the age of reason because articulating Aristotelian metaphysics, personal finance, and a work ethic is just too much work. Teenagers can do what they want once they are into puberty because, in the liberal world, heterosexuality is not morally preferable to homosexuality and birth control will blot out any mistakes made anyway. When the kid graduates from high school, college is in order because that is what looks good to other liberal parents. Whoever can get the most enlightened college degree wins! There is no guidance for the adult-child through their 20's because the liberal parent has not matured past their early 20's and has no wisdom to offer. Even if they did, the child has to live their own life and that's groovy, man.

White racism is literally the worst thing ever and explains all of the disparate outcomes ever.

Liberal parents are terrified of their children having ethnic consciousness because it means their kids will start to think in a nationalist or tribalist manner and start outcompeting other people. Liberalism is all about suicidality. People ought not to think back on their histories to find examples of excellence and greatness. People should not identify with Christopher Columbus, Hernando Cortez, Charlemagne, Douglas MacArthur, Abraham Lincoln, or the Founding Fathers. All conflict needs to sanitized so that everyone can get back to being in agreeable moods they characterize as "empathy and compassion." You are supposed to identify with a house plant or a house cat or some hungry African child. People are routinely parented this way and *who they are* goes from something tremendous, noble, adventurous, innocent, and automatically, naturally protective of that innocence to a houseplant. "Racism" just happens to be the animating principle of all successful cultures, including places like Japan and South Korea, but white men are the ones most readily demoralized by nagging. Rather than a love of beauty or an appreciation of excellence, people in their identities are reduced to hating white man having the outlook of a houseplant.

Sometimes I'm *sexy* and I love orgasming.

Bad parenting treats the sexual development of children as a slow admission process into the global orgy of nations and peoples. Premarital sex is no different than marital sex because, "Lol, you believe in God. I believe in Science." The liberal retains no curiosity as to why, even absent a deity and a religious order, pre-marital sex would be problematic for a lifelong vow a person takes with another...let alone why a person would conceivably want to devote their lives to someone else in mind and body. Sex becomes a seduction, rather than a sincere commitment. Sex is used as a tool of manipulation and control instead of a procreative act where peoples highest selves are joined in union for the benefit of the next generation. Since liberal sex requires seduction, being *sexy* is a social value. Here comes the lipstick. Here comes the "gainz" at the gym. People focus on being desirable meat puppets to one another instead of improving their moral and spiritual conditions. Or people give up on having desirable bodies altogether, cause their parents never exercised with them growing up, and they place extra emphasis on their desire itself as justification for easy sex. There is no shortage of emotionally immature (synonymous with "liberal") sickly skinny men and obese women copulating like pigs.

The need to be "sexy" is a primitive way of admitting either that one was not taught to appreciate one's own body by one's parents, that one did not feel adored and venerated as a child by the parent of the opposite sex, or that one had to turn to seduction in order to withdraw physical affection as a child. Daughters learn to seduce their fathers, if their fathers are unsatisfied perverts. Sons learn to bolster their mother's sexualities, if their mothers chose weak, undesirable men. The family works in a system and a deficit between the parents will leak out onto the children.

The love of orgasming is the love of worldly pleasure. We are not allowed to frame things this way because psychotherapeutic language wholly pervades our culture. There is no shame in coming for the purposes of procreation. There is no shame in masturbating once in a long while because of genuinely felt physical desire (and *not* to mood manage). The great challenge of parenting a teenager is to help them gear their profound hormonal states toward self-discovery, existential adventure, and moral formation. A healthy parent stands and delivers from standards, not the weird, neurotic "okay-making" that psychology concerns itself with. The psychotherapeutic worldview debases people because in their search to destigmatize the orgasm, they lose sight of standards that tell us what sex is for. Sex is not recreational. Liberal people make it that way and then they use pop psychology to find "acceptance" from Science or to browbeat Christians with, "You know, I just *don't* feel shame about it, no matter how much I soul-search!" As if these people are not love cripples already that have lost sight of a standard Christianity has long inspired people to *endeavor to* with *difficulty*. Emerging from one's teenage years without an addiction to worldly pleasure is *difficult* but not impossible. People who need to orgasm to manage their difficult internal states are not in a position to provide insight and instruction to young people on matters of sex. Being a slave to desire and impulse is a cornerstone of the liberal, "Who am I?"

"Good enough" is okay. Once I reach the average, I can stop trying.

Mediocre parenting produces mediocre results. Bad parenting produces bad results. Parents have to *want* to be good parents in order to become good parents. Through reason and evidence, standards for parenting have to posited. When standards are established, a parent strives to meet those standards. Their level of effort and care is transmitted to the children. Most people, if they have pre-frontal cortex function, and that is a big *IF*, *decide* to become parents and therefore have some conception that it entails a set of responsibilities. "Good enough" is the operating procedure. "Good enough" places parents firmly in the pack but not on either end of the spectrum of excellent to terrible, where they would be noticed for their excellence or awfulness. People do not want to risk social ostracism, either because they value the sanctity of their children's development so much that they are willing to be at odds with the community or because they are so terrible the authorities will come take their children away. This attitude is conveyed to the children, who grow up to go for the middle of the pack somewhere themselves. People's average attitudes about their children become instilled in the children as value-assessments of themselves.

I want to be rich but that's so much hard work. It's like a mystery to me. Eat the rich!

People with insecure attachments to their parents (for more on Attachment Theory, check out my book *Dead West Walking*) are instilled with an all-pervading, in-the-bone-marrow sense of not being good enough. There is no heartbreak like the heartbreak of an innocent child. As I wrote in my song *Bring Out Your Dead*[50]: a child's heart you can't unbreak. People who achieve their full potential in adulthood, more often than not, had parents who safeguarded their essential potential. We are all familiar with the rags-to-riches stories of famous entertainers, politicians, and businessmen who had parents that *believed* in them unfailingly. What happens with these people is that they learn to overcome and outperform their own parents' failings or the broader community's bigotries as a way of *believing* in the sanctity of the family. They were nurtured into leadership through their parents' *belief* in them and in adulthood take command in order to put the entire family system on a higher track. With

---

[50] https://www.youtube.com/watch?v=Krpzrx__dRM

peaceful parenting, we can take these inspiring success stories and add the component of ending intergenerational trauma.

Our children *are* good enough for us. They are a reflection of us and we were born with amazing potential. We come to feel bitter and disappointed with life if we were thwarted from achieving our potential and thus learned to thwart ourselves. AND, if we are not taught to deal with life's inevitable and occasional disappointments, we cope badly and feel disillusioned. This personal loss becomes intellectualized into socialism or Communism, which are ideologies of envy and revenge. Before the Industrial Revolution, the truth is that man was locked into a death battle with nature. From nature, man has carved out civilization, food supplies against famines, antidotes against antigens, and air control against temperature extremes. There have been trials and tribulations along the way. We have not come this far because man's productive enterprise is essentially bad. We are fortunate for the sacrifice of our forefathers. We honor them by seeing in our children the good that is to come and the potential that lies within.

Identity

Identity is not the dirty word that some big brained centrists would have you believe. Identity is simply a fact of people's existences. Through clear thinking, we can help the parts of our identity that are malleable and learn to have fruitful relationships with people who have identities different than our own. Ethics transcends tribes and allows people to get on with living in the age of mass communication.

A healthy identity is based on virtue and a respect for the parts of ourselves that we were born with. A person cannot help that they were born this or that ethnicity, this or that skin color, but what they do with this fact has largely been left up to Marxists professors in Europe and the United States. We can do better. With peaceful parenting, we can take into account the parts of our children's identities they cannot help, such as being born white or something like this, and help them to be self-knowledgeable of these inherent qualities so that when they come into contact with other people, they will be prepared to engage in win-win negotiations and fun, for goodness sakes! The way this is done is by conveying to our children that there is such thing as *objective truth* in this world. You cannot argue against objective truth because in saying that there is no such as objective truth, you are attempting to posit an objective truth. Circular logic like this leads to unnecessary suffering. The foundation of peaceful parenting is rooted in a respect for objective truth. This raises our children up above moral relativism, cultural relativism, science dogmatism, Marxism, and so forth. As it relates to identity, when children know there are universal truths, they can come to appreciate the good parts of their home cultures and tendencies of their ethnic kinsmen while administrating morally to the struggling or even evil aspects. Objective truth takes the confusion out of issues of identity that so many young people are struggling with today. What if a young person is born bi-racial, as increasing numbers of people are because of globalism? Rather than feel at odds with themselves and eventually resentful of one side or another, this person can come to terms with their feelings of identification with separate and sometimes conflicting groups. This balance is *so important* in the world that is coming because Marxism promotes the exact opposite. Marxism tells people to be resentful of history and to tear down any chance there is at successful, long-term negotiation. Identity is at the heart of people's value systems, despite our best efforts to inculcate everyone with universal values derived from philosophy or Christianity. We need to be savvy so that we do not load our children up with principles for thinking that only worked in homogenous, non-globalized societies.

Marxism has been particularly successful in rewriting the identities of minority groups in the United States. Marxism took people who were family-oriented, cognizant of jurisprudent expectations and their intrinsic value, Christ-seeking, and work-oriented and turned them into welfare-depending, fatherless, ideologically aggrieved foot soldiers for corporate consumption and the mega therapeutic state. Marxism has lied to black people by telling them that had colonialism not happened, Africans would be using energy weapons and flying vehicles on a regular basis. Marxism has lied to Hispanics by telling them that land was once "stolen" from them and that the only path to justice lies through using the state to "steal back" land from the white man. The lies go on and on. Marxism says that to be whatever shade of non-white, you have to hate white people and be aggrieved. Marxism says that to be white, you have to hate yourself and live in a quasi-suicidal state at all times. People take this indoctrination seriously and encode it into their identities. Marxism, liberalism, race theory, liberal progressivism, whatever you want to call it, knows that if you can convince people that their inalterable features *must* mean automatically that a person has to destroy civilization, evil triumphs and good is destroyed forever. There are millions of black people walking around America with their identities saying to them, "I am black; therefore, I am oppressed." This flies in the face of empirical truth. America is the shining city on the hill. There has never been a better time or place to be born as a black person, or a person of any other race for that matter, than America. Marxism is extremely careful to not tell white people, "You are white; therefore, you are oppressed." Yet, because it weaponizes every identity group outside of white people against white people, Marxism is bringing about a world where white people *are* oppressed. This has significant bearing on peaceful parenting because if we cannot tell our children the truth about "the score" that Marxism has run up, largely through the lying corporate media, we cannot empower them to understand the problems that will be set at their feet, whether they are white, bi-racial, brown, or any other color. If our children do not understand that the world of ideological pettiness depicted to them through the awe-inspiring power of the media, Hollywood, social media, and other platforms is largely a lie, they will inculcate the same lies into their identities that everyone else is falling prey to. The truth is that Western Civilization after the American Civil War and before the European Civil War was a place of unprecedented international peace, economic and social prosperity, demographic growth for the right reasons, adventure, art, and innovation. Were people to identify with this, as opposed to the psychosis of Marvel movies or Nike commercials, the world would be a whole lot better off and racial struggles would seem distant and alien.

Our inalterable qualities have been ideologized and turned against us and one another. In our educative responsibilities to our children, we need to place an emphasis on the glories of Western Civilization as a unifying, ethical experiment unrivaled in world history and on the enjoyable facets of our respective races, civilizations, and religions. Prior to the 1980's, *National Geographic* had it mostly correct. "Look at these interesting statues these people on the other side of the globe made. That is rather interesting, isn't it? Look how these people pair bond and resolve disputes in their village. What works? What doesn't?" This dispassionate, anthropological attitude about the broader world outside of Western Civilization was derived from an identity wholly separate from Marxism. Some people say we need a "return to tradition". This book posits that traditional values served *everyone*, universally, and that we need a value system that also inoculates our children from Marxism. Marxism has only worked because it preyed upon the envy that groups outside of Western Civilization felt *toward* Western Civilization. So what if air conditioning was invented somewhere first? So what if one group of people built skyscrapers while another was stuck building grass thatch huts? These facts should be of service to us, not something to be butthurt and vindictive about. Nobody, in conventional circles, dares bat an eye when a certain group in the Middle East makes audacious land grabs at the expense of others, namely families and children. If we cannot be universally butthurt about every single actual aggression from one group toward another, then Marxism falls flat on its face and we need a better value system to introduce to identity. People who learn to love what is great about what they were *born into* and, even more importantly, how objective truth actually empowers all people everywhere are people that can greet the world in an inquisitive, socially deft, and judicious manner. In this spirit, I am American and you are, let us say, Filipino, and that is *okay*. We have plenty of common ground yet we are distinct, often for reasons outside of immediate control, and we are highly likely to be in competition with one another when the rubber really meets the road. It is okay. Let us talk. Let us break bread. Liberal progressivism unnecessarily and unfairly disrupts the equation by confusing both parties in different ways. This has to stop. We need to meet as gentlemen, not crazed butthurt babies and suicidal degenerates.

Self-knowledge is the knowledge of what is true about ourselves. Marxism is a perverting and mutating force. People confuse the Marxism they have been indoctrinated with for who they really are. Bad parenting sets the stage for Marxism, as we saw with the list of examples of liberal parenting and the attitudes they imbue into the child. The truth about children is that children are wonderful, curious, empiricism-driven creatures that have significant developmental needs. Children are not civil rights marchers or Starbucks window-breakers. Children are not pedophile financiers of NGOs or nervous bureaucrats doing everything in their power to destroy strait-laced people. Children are made this way, especially the ones that come from more moral societies. Children from low intelligence societies that were in a primitive state *before* Communism was even a thing tend to have more struggles with civilized behavior but until parenting across the globe is totally and completely corrected to peaceful parenting, we will not fully know the difference between our societies. We can only work with best working theories. We can reasonably infer that violence as a social tool more readily occurs in the natural instincts of some people versus other people. This should not be a point of psychotic hysteria but simply a best working theory that allows us to move on to higher considerations. When you think about it, much of Western society has been dumbed down and indoctrinated to the point where we are all navel gazing on this best working theory because the word "racist" is thrown around like popcorn at a failed movie premiere.

Instincts and Refinement

Once we can clear Marxist nonsense from our internal systems, we can take a more accurate survey of ourselves. Kids tend to want to be moral. Remove Marxism, corporal punishment, shaming and scolding and suddenly kids are:

-assertive about property rights and generous when they have more than they need

-energetic and creative

-curious about their higher selves and unseen dimensions of the world

-sweet, loving, and gentle

-enterprising and negotiating

These are not perfect maxims because some kids who have not ever seen hitting or been hit themselves will hit things when they are frustrated. There are some children born more aggressive than others.[51] We do not know perfectly each individual child's exact potential but we clear the deck as much as possible when we peacefully parent. We take away our own private bigotries from the equation. Children will have unique tendencies, some of them downstream from their inalterable qualities.

---

[51] https://en.wikipedia.org/wiki/Brunner_syndrome

Right now, we do not have perfect knowledge of what tendencies are ancestral and heritable. We do know that if you hit a kid or screw with their self-knowledge process by indoctrinating them, you get more of the same.

A self-knowledgeable child is a child who is enjoined by their parent to self-reflect. You start this process with the child when they are young by bringing their attention on how different behaviors have different consequences. They grab a bug too hard and the bug is squished and dead. This is not cause for hysterics and disappointment from the parent. The parent should not *steal* the emotions of the child by being upset or disappointed. Rather, allow the child to feel disappointed. Mirror back to the child what the child is feeling through a matter-of-fact explanation of the action and consequence that just played out. We feel disappointed when something happens that we did not want to happen. We wanted to keep playing with the bug but it died. Or it was a dangerous bug, our parent killed it, and we do not yet understand danger all that well because we have not experienced much physical pain in our lives. All of this can be explained. Another example of early lessons on self-knowledge comes from sleep routines. Some children are confused by sleep and they do not like the sensation of falling asleep. They fight against it. As their capacity for understanding us improves, we help them to identify when they are feeling sleeping, what it feels like in their bodies, and how sleep helps them to be happy.

The basic mechanism of slowing things down for the child and calling their attention to their bodily sensations and internal states is what develops self-knowledge in a child. The culture of addiction prevalent across the globe today calls for people to *speed up*, disregard internal experiences in favor of temporary distractions, and above all costs to idealize what is wrong so that criminality can continue unchecked. The funny thing about teaching a child to slow down and figure out what is going on is that eventually they become remarkably efficient at this and they then barrel through life and cause all sorts of problems for the people who propagate the culture of addiction. Our instincts are accurate. We are descended from thousands of generations of people who tested themselves on a *daily* basis against giant predators, pestilences, periods of famine, and other tribes who warred and schemed against one another. Those who erred died. Nowadays we generally do not live in such an immediate way but the instincts have remained. We can tune into those instincts and they help us in our daily living replete with air conditioning (can you tell I love controlled air?), supply chains, and social media.

Barring congenital defects, our children's instincts are firmly intact when they come into the world. Self-knowledge reinforces those instincts with conceptual knowledge. Sometimes our children's instincts will clash with our parenting. We have to slow down in these moments and understand how to help our children harmonize their instincts with consistent, higher ideals. We can only do this if we remain committed ourselves to self-knowledge throughout our adult lives into old age.

Punishment is the opposite of self-knowledge. Punishment is the choice to inflict pain as a corrective force over simple, matter of fact reasoning. Punishment against innocent children is inappropriate. Punishment is only appropriate between adults and in a judicial capacity, as it is not the responsibility of adults to have to correct the immoral behavior of criminals. Western parenting does not turn children into criminals. Just as (ideally) a philosopher in his adult life deals with difficult experiences by self-reflecting, so too do children learn best. Our captains of industry, greatest military leaders (which have not even existed in a couple generations), cultural icons, and Christian teachers have succeeded *despite* any punishment they imposed upon themselves internally, punishment they learned in childhood. Punishment makes children incoherent. They lose their zeal to reason through life's difficulties. Punishment corrodes children. Great careers can be built on top of corroded foundations but as mentioned earlier in this book, that is a total roll of the dice.

Children do not have the capacities of adults. Kind of obvious but it is important to state for this next bit. Children need refinement. Eventually, they yearn for it. Children need parents as a tether to higher ideals because they can and do get lost in their emotional states. Getting bit by a puppy hurts, therefore the child cries. The child cries and cries. The parent needs to intervene and soothe the child so the child can learn how to deal with puppies once the pain has subsided. To touch upon a point from earlier, some children do not like the physical sensations of feeling sleepy. Thus, they cry and cry and get lost in their crying. The parent must, however primitively but without aggression, intervene and, over time, refine the child's conceptual capacities so that falling asleep *makes sense*. Neglect, being the primary form of abuse, often has to do with simply leaving a child to wallow in their initial reactions to difficulties in the world. Yes, losing the Pinewood Derby or getting crappy candy when you go trick-or-treating are negative experiences but to be *left* in those experiences is neglect on the part of the parent. Same goes from pooping in your diaper all the way up to getting turned down for a job application and beyond. As parents, we need to be in tune with our children's instincts but always refining and honing their conceptual capacities in a way that does not disrupt their instincts. The first voice is the right voice.

Spouse Selection

Excellence in spouse selection starts with knowing the relevant facts. In the West, public school completely fails to empower young people with what they need to know in order to choose well. The vague criteria for choosing a spouse runs something along the lines of finding someone who bolsters you in your comfort, someone who likes the same brands and hobbies as you, and someone who you *like* or lust after. People caught in the momentum of their childhoods, and without moral instruction in early adulthood, tend to gravitate toward people who remind them of their parent of the opposite sex. After all, the mental grooves are well in place at this point. A man who had a timid, nervous mother will end up with a timid, nervous wife. A woman who had a cowardly, TV-watching father will end up with an Internet-addicted, vaguely libertarian husband. Repeat ad nauseum. We are bound to our histories until we bring self-knowledge and Christian courage into the equation. We do better than average when we face down the truth about ourselves, about the sorry state of the dating market, and about the relevant facts that inform superior decision making.

The prevailing and most relevant fact to the question of spouse selection that we will cover is the concept of the body count – the number of partners a person has had. From HuffPost, of all places, we read:

A widely reported new study claims that people -- especially women -- who have multiple sexual partners before tying the knot, report unhappier marriages down the line. The study comes to us from The National Marriage Project, based off research from two University of Denver professors, Galena K. Rhoades and Scott M. Stanley, who looked at relationship data collected from 2007 to 2008 of 1,000 unmarried Americans ages 18 to 34. During the following five years, 418 of the participants got married.

Rhoades and Stanley took a closer look at those marriages to see if factors, including participants' sexual past, played a role in current marital quality. Couples' relationship quality was measured using a four-item version of the Dyadic Adjustment Scale, focusing on relationship happiness, thoughts about separation, frequency of confiding in one another, and a general item about how well things are going (the full scale, however, contains 32 items).

According to researchers, the 23 percent of participants who only had sex with their spouse prior to getting hitched reported higher quality marriages versus those who had other past sexual partners as well.

They claim this finding is especially true for women, writing in the report, 'We further found that the more sexual partners a woman had had before marriage, the less happy she reported her marriage to be.'[52]

Remember the controversial line earlier in this book, "Sex is not for recreation"? Yeah, not so controversial now, is it? The research is clear: stick to as few partners as possible, *if* you want marital satisfaction. The ideal has and always will be to have one sex partner your entire life. Women are particularly impacted in terms of marital satisfaction when it comes to number of partners:

> This research brief shows that the relationship between divorce and the number of sexual partners women have prior to marriage is complex. I explore this relationship using data from the three most recent waves of the National Survey of Family Growth (NSFG) collected in 2002, 2006-2010, and 2011-2013. For women marrying since the start of the new millennium:
>
> -Women with 10 or more partners were the most likely to divorce, but this only became true in recent years;

---

[52] https://www.huffpost.com/entry/more-sexual-partners-unhappy-marriage_n_5698440

-Women with 3-9 partners were less likely to divorce than women with 2 partners; and,

-Women with 0-1 partners were the least likely to divorce.[53]

The percentage of women that are having 10+ partners has risen by 800% in the past 40 years. Bad things happen to society when women are unable to bond with men, due to riding the carousel of easy sex. Feminism has put it into women's minds that men are expendable, attendant to serve women's needs above all else, and that there is a Brad Pitt waiting for every woman, just around the corner.

Women are the gatekeepers of sex. The undeniable fact is that they are the ones to choose when the couple has sex. Women are choosing for looks and risky behavior, instead of the ability to provide and stability. Since the advent of birth control, women's incentives have completely changed:

Women could begin to have the number of children they *wished* to have. But over time the wide uptake of contraception has functioned to split what once was a relatively unified mating market into two quite distinct components. By "relatively unified" I simply mean that the majority of paired sexual activity among unmarried persons was conducted in and during the search for a mate, that is, someone to marry. Sex didn't necessarily mean marriage, but relationship security was often a value and a precursor to sex. In a survey of Americans conducted in 1970—which interviewed over 3,000 adults, some of whom were born before 1900—54 percent of the oldest men but only 7 percent of the oldest women reported having had premarital intercourse. With each successive cohort, those numbers rose,

---

[53] https://ifstudies.org/blog/counterintuitive-trends-in-the-link-between-premarital-sex-and-marital-stability

until 89 percent of men and 63 percent of women in the youngest cohort (born in 1940–49) reported premarital sex. This doesn't mean that our grandparents never messed around—whatever that meant to them. But in general, the average woman could and did count on seeing evidence of commitment before sex. If she didn't—and got pregnant—her family might step into the role of guarantor.[54]

Society went from men being in charge of family size to women *choosing* family size. Women have been placed in the driver's seat of selection by unchristian, birth control scientists. They are choosing to have less children, which leads to less happiness, and choosing to have more careers. Since they do not have to face the "risk" of pregnancy, women dabble more often in casual sex and they are encouraged to do so by the mainstream media.

When prospective peaceful parents begin to understand the corrosive nature of easy sex and how birth control has tilted the tables unnaturally, better choices can be made. Casual sex burns away the foundations of organized society. Promiscuous men create feminists by putting bonding hormones in the women and then backing away, which is the same as heartbreak. Women become embittered, angry, lose their ability to trust, oftentimes collect little apartment dogs, drink wine, and vote for Democrats. Promiscuous women create incels. An incel is an involuntarily celibate male. The incel phenomena is in full swing now. The establishment has worked overtime to depict incels as radical, toxic, white supremacist school shooters but the establishment is only doing this for political gain. The establishment seeks to rehabilitate immigrant rapists and to let them out again to rape more after only the lightest of prison sentences. This is because of liberal feminist rape fantasies. When the home population of the West has anger toward women, because

---

[54] https://link.springer.com/article/10.1007/s12115-012-9592-2

women are only giving sex to Brad Pitt types, the home population must be made to suffer even further. The establishment is *terrified* of any unifying cause among white men because "Hitler 2.0". This is a hyper-hot-button issue because feminists are running places like Western Europe, Canada, New Zealand, and America into the ground. Men who show any self-awareness about being sexually disenfranchised by feminism must be profiled by Deep State agents as domestic terrorists. This is a case of guilty conscience by the establishment. The truth is much different.

Incels, by and large and aside from a few that psychiatrists have filled with homicidal-ideating medications, are simply sexually disenfranchised men who are self-aware. All the establishment has to point to on why "incel bad" is Elliot Rodger, who was on elephant grade psychiatric medication, and one stupid idiot immigrant in Toronto who shot someone and said he was "incel" once on Facebook. The fact is that incels are not bad for engaging in jokes, discussion, and memes centered around their plight. Their nihilism is actually rather easy to tolerate if you are equipped the relevant facts. Deep State fragility seeks to criminalize their unique point of view. Incels can be enfranchised once again, pulled back from whatever "ledge" they reside, and helped to become masculine leaders in their community. But this comes at the expense of the therapeutic super state administrated by such tyrants as Angela Merkel, Justin Trudeau, and Emanuel Macron. This author would be placed in jail in any of these defunct states by intelligence services for the free words of this previous paragraph. Thankfully, we still live in Trump's America, for the time being, and free speech can illuminate the most provocative corners of the human experience. Being an incel does not automatically necessitate being filled with revenge fantasies, murderous ideations, and actual plans for retribution against women. The numbskull jackboots of the socialist state would have you believe otherwise because it allows them to jail dissidents against the globo-homo order. Men should be consumptive, acquisitive homosexuals, not self-aware of their disenfranchisement! Globalist governors would like nothing more than to open up the slaughter of a few more Ruby Ridges to make an example out of disenfranchised white males. This is wrong. We need de-escalation on *all* sides. The fundamentals of excellent spouse selection offer the steps we need to get away from further psychotic state intervention into the sexual market place. In words the intelligence agencies will understand: this book seeks to *de-radicalize* incels, and that is accepting the premise that incels are somehow radical anyway.

Both men and women are complicit in destroying the foundations of the nuclear family unit. Each of us must be the change we wish to see in the world. According to a study done by Choi, Wong, and Fong:

> To the best of our knowledge, this was the first study to examine the association between the use of dating apps and sexual health in a sample of heterosexual, bisexual and homosexual subjects. The present study found that the use of dating apps was associated with having more sexual partners, having unprotected sexual intercourse with more sexual partners, an increased likelihood of having inconsistent condom use and an increased likelihood of not having used a condom the last time the subject had sexual intercourse. It appeared that dating apps tended to skew their users toward risky sexual encounters.

> More than half of the study sample used dating apps suggesting that dating apps are popular among college students. After controlling for sociodemographic factors, users of dating apps had 87% more likely to have sexual intercourse experience than nonusers. There are at least two possible explanations. First, the nature of dating apps with their convenience, accessibility and mobility can facilitate sexual encounters. Second, people who are

sexually active and intend to look for sexual encounters in the first place may be drawn to dating apps to look for sexual activities. This merits further investigation to understand the causal relationship between using dating apps and the initiation of sexual intercourse.[55]

We need to understand that dating apps are risky ventures for users. There are success stories everywhere but there are far more casual sex stories. The dating apps do not make efforts to dissuade recreational sex. In fact, they benefit from the addictive nature of recreational sex. They are incentivized to hook people in. Cigarette packs carry warning labels. Dating apps do not. College, combined with dating apps, is a particularly potent cocktail for easy sex.

In the age of totalitarian COVID-19 government lockdowns where police break up house parties, family reunions, and commit human rights violations by blocking Christian prayer services, meeting people in-person has become a difficult prospect – especially outside of the United States. The pivot away from dating apps means leveraging personal relationships and networks in order to meet the right person. We have become overdependent, generally speaking, on government and corporate solutions to personal challenges. The Church brought together successful spousal partnerships better than any Indian programmer crammed into a tiny apartment with fifteen other people in a coastal American city ever could. We need to encourage our young people out of liberal arts colleges, away from the cancerous dating apps (especially the ones that place an emphasis on casual encounters like Tinder), and *talk* to one another on a regular basis in-person, despite what buffoon governments think we should be doing. Who knows? The COVID-19 lockdowns in the United States will likely end soon, especially if Democrats are prevented from

---

[55] https://www.ncbi.nlm.nih.gov/pmc/articles/PMC5102411/

stealing the election. Let us not date this book too much by focusing on some bioweapon released by globalists.

By now we have well established that pornography, casual sex, feminism, and birth control lead to terrible outcomes. So, don't do these things! Body counts hurt both men and women. Men and women alike need to practice abstinence and save themselves from marriage. Instead of watching pornography, people need to fill their heads with books, self-reflection, Christian prayer, and values that are antithetical to feminism – such as traditionalism or peaceful parenting. Women should try living without birth control to see how much more in-tune they become with their hormonal cycles, how the changed incentive environment helps them to approach men differently, and what happens to their ambitions for family size. Women *are* the gatekeepers currently but more and more of them are discovering that the side effects of birth control are too much to bear. Side effects are the number one reason cited for birth control discontinuation.[56]

Given an overview of some of the relevant facts most pertinent to today's dating market, that would be taught to people by schools in a just society, we can begin to get honest about who it is that we are going to choose to peacefully parent with. There is no perfect wife or husband out there just a phone call away. Marriage is a bond that, when done right, engenders virtue over time. We cannot let the ideal perfect get in the way of the pragmatic good, though standards should always inform and improve our decision-making.

Let us start with what men should be looking for. At a baseline, men should be looking for a woman with a low body count, preferably women who are virgins. Can you hear the shrieks of feminists yet? It is true though. The highest chance a man has at having a satisfied wife is

[56] https://pubmed.ncbi.nlm.nih.gov/22865164/

marrying one who has had one or no sexual partners at all. Obviously, this cannot be the first question a man springs on a woman in their first interaction but it is *vital* information to gather in the early going. Women who are virgins are most easily found at the age of 18 and then beyond that at Christian religious institutions that still espouse some measure of conservative values. Men can also learn to spot virgins by noting the absence of piercings, substance abuse, tattoos, apartment dogs, and other accumulations that are markers of trauma and evil in the woman's dating profile pictures. There is a lot of truth to the notion of female purity but some despoiled women understand this and thus festoon themselves in the appearance of female purity. These women are overcompensating. The simple question, "How many sex partners have you had?" will let you know if her show of purity is sincere or if it is compensatory and long after the fact. You do not need to inherit the mess another man made. Not every man is going to get a virgin or a woman with a body count under three but neither do you need to rationalize yourself into a woman who is an out and out liability.

People of both sexes who want to peacefully parent need to know their Sexual Market Value. To keep it brief, this is your score of attractiveness on a scale of one to ten. Men are valued for their ability provide, protect, their physical appearance, and their leadership abilities. Women are valued on their fertility, their looks (which are connected to their fertility) and their ability as mothers. Men can raise their scores by exercising, making more money, and by integrating themselves further into the fraternal order. Women can raise their scores by marrying young, exercising, and staying out of debt or even ensuring they come into a marriage with a dowry of some kind. One's sexual market value score is an age-old assessment common to American culture. It is not some grand mystery that whole books need to be devoted to. When a prospective peaceful parent knows his or her sexual market value, he or she can find a spouse within a point or half point of the score. Men who are tens should not be getting with fours. Women who are tens should be getting with men who are eights or higher. This is not complicated science. This is something we all intuit at a gut level. Accurate self-knowledge means we know "the score". You know your score, you aim accordingly. The higher your score, the more people will work to convince you to settle. The lower your score, the more society will disregard you. People overinflate their scores *all the time* out of a sense of personal insecurity. There is no shame in being ugly or somewhat ugly. You can always raise your score this way and that, especially if you are a man. The sooner you know what your value is to other people, the sooner you can aim your sights correctly. As mentioned earlier, not every man is going to get a virgin. Not every woman is going to get a stellar provider. There will be people who settle and then feel regret the rest of their lives. There are people who will overachieve and then feel jealous the rest of their lives. Keeping an accurate tab on your own score and what prospects you are reviewing gives you the best chance at avoiding these problems.

One other major thing to mention with sexual market value is that there is a giant glut of women from about a score of 4 to a score of 7.75 that think they are entitled to an 8 or higher. This is because their heads are full of media and their bodies are full of birth control. The average looking male in the United States has been stripped of his birthright by feminism, etc. In today's dating market, men who are average looking have to expend extraordinary effort, compared to above average looking men, in order to convince an average woman to lower her expectations. Women are flocking to top tier men, the top tier men are fornicating them and forgetting them (making feminists in the process), and then the women are collecting kitty cats and raging at Donald Trump while hoping student loan forgiveness becomes federalized. This cannot continue. It takes a certain amount of understanding and patience to help average women out of this dating trap. The sooner an average man gets it in his mind to *guide* a woman out of this trap, the easier his prospects become. People, especially in the United States, want to be good. They have just been lied to for so long that the dating market has become completely lopsided.

Aside from the body count question, men do well to get these following questions answered:

How is the woman's relationship to her parents?

A close relationship to her parents means that they respected her in childhood by preparing her to be a mother and wife. They imparted to her the practical skills she will need to keep a home as a homemaker. She may have been classically trained in piano, singing, or in dressmaking. Perhaps she had an administrative or people-facing role in the family business. She was raised to understand *why* socialism is evil, that you cannot get things out of men for free, and that only strong, virtuous men are worth gravitating toward. A woman may feel she has a close relationship to her liberal parents but this is completely an accident of what they did right in their sober moments than any leftist parenting philosophy they practiced. Stockholm Syndrome is the norm in liberal families. The parents use the child's dependence on them in order to brainwash the child into the evil cult of liberalism. Evil parents double down when they are called out on their abuses. There are a rare few liberal-*leaning* parents who did enough despite their rotten ideologies that they can weather honest criticism later, reform themselves to a sufficient degree, and still be productive, useful members of their daughters' extended families.

If a woman is not close to her parents, it is because her parents failed. This does not necessarily mean she is a failed prospect for the man but it does mean that she will have attachment issues that will need to be worked through in a conscious manner. By definition, a woman who is past the age of 20 and into a career is not close to her parents. She has gone too far out of the home and too far into the marketplace to say that she experienced great parenting. This is an ideal standard and 95% of women in the world, and their parents, will fail this standard. This is how pervasive the myth of liberalism has become. We should not be autistic and cut people off for not meeting this standard. Rather, we should help guide people to excellence by healing the family and telling the truth to people about the quality of their relationships.

What are this woman's outward markers of trauma, corruption, or evil?

The major ones were mentioned earlier: piercings, substance abuse, tattoos, and pets. The piercings may have been done to her when she was a child. It is not right to inflict pain upon a child. Children should not be getting pierced by metal. Some women get more and more piercings as they age and become spiritually compromised. The first place a woman generally gets pierced after her ears is her nose, usually a small stud. Much beyond this and she is showing irreparable corruption. Women who have their erogenous zones pierced should be avoided at all costs. Men should also not be getting piercings as they are a sign of submission to pain. The same goes for tattoos. A woman may have a tattoo or two from her early adulthood that she regrets but fundamentally, she has spiritually branded herself and it will be the man's burden for the rest of his days looking after her not to indulge in unkind dominance of her. Tattoos on women should be avoided. Visible tattoos are a red flag. It is hard to meet the standards of peaceful parenting between two unmarked people, let alone to bring in a woman who suffered so much from low self-esteem that she put a mark on herself.

Substance abuse is a red flag. Remember, men who have a lower sexual market value will have to take on some of these problems. Substance abuse is entirely correlated to childhood trauma. Women who have substance abuse issues should not be dating. Instead, they should be in quiet cloisters in the countryside removed from men. Substance abuse has been normalized in popular culture. A coffee every single day or on even half of days is substance abuse. This is because caffeine disrupts a person's connection to the most spiritual and artistic aspects of themselves and puts them squarely in a worker's mindset. More than a drink or two of alcohol a month is minor substance abuse. Use of marijuana is substance abuse. Psychiatric medication for mood disorders is substance abuse. So is regular use of sleep aids. More than a single sugary treat a week is substance abuse. Women should not be smoking cigarettes as they are an oral fixation. Overeating and unhealthy eating is probably the most common substance abuse of them all.

Unmarried women should not own pets. Pets are a proxy for children. Women need to be having children. Women who own pets, volunteer as pet "fosters", walk dogs, dog-sit, etc. develop their maternal habits around beasts instead of children. Their personalities take on a hard, masculine edge that is wholly inappropriate to women. Men tame beasts, not women. Only through consistent interaction with actual children, early in a woman's adulthood and teenage development, can a woman develop the supple nature that is most appropriate for the disposition a woman needs to be a good mother. Dogs are a pitiful proxy for children. Cats are, by their nature, schizophrenic and disloyal and cat owners eventually take on these characteristics. Cats are street animals that control rodent populations. Some women own rats or reptiles, which spread disease or kill infants. Owning reptiles is a sign of extreme childhood abuse. Reptiles are unnatural to Western Civilization and are incapable of serving a mammalian purpose. People need to bond to people, first and foremost, and then they can have pets within the context of a family and only up to a certain point. A family should not own more than two dogs, unless for breeding purposes. Families should not own cats as house pets as cats are fundamentally disloyal and will serve as an example to the children that it is acceptable to be uprooted from the family unit.

Women should not be owning dogs specifically because dogs serve as proxies to men. They fulfill one of the core duties of men, which is to protect. A woman can get some guard dog breed, treat the dog like a boyfriend or husband in her most private moments, and forgo the challenges of pair-bonding with an actual adult male human until a time of her choosing. Men correct women's thinking but dogs do not. Dogs apply no interhuman pressure on a woman's personality. Dogs obey and protect the hand that feeds them. Women pervert this obedience because they had inadequate fathers and cannot personally face how their fathers were inadequate. A woman who had an adequate father will turn to the loving protection of a virtuous man, early on in her adulthood. Protective dogs only become a necessity because of multiculturalism and the presence of foreigner men from rape cultures.

Is this woman in debt? What is the woman's relationship to money?

Women are not competent to make the money decisions men make, as covered earlier in the book. A man needs to know if a woman is in debt early on in the dating because debt lowers a woman's sexual market value. The debt she carries can, and often does, lower her sexual market value to the point where she is no longer a worthy prospect of the man (given the man is out of debt and a capable provider). Sometimes both a man and woman are in debt. The man needs to weigh the amount of the debt against the time the loans will be paid back and how much of the woman's fertility will be used setting things right. This is the great evil of student loans. There is no university course of study available to a woman, outside of medical training later in life, that is worth a woman going into debt for during her fertility window. Women do not need to be participants in the market economy. Women are at a disadvantage when they do participate in the economy but the losses are sublimated into the emotional lives of their children, which do not fully reveal themselves until the children are teenagers.

A woman's relationship to money is important because it is indicative of her spending and saving habits as a wife. If she carries consumer debt, she will likely be the kind to spend extra on shopping trips. She will buy this and that on Amazon. A man needs to be prepared for these habits and work with the woman to whatever degree he needs to until there is marital satisfaction around spending. A woman may be the kind to squirrel away money. This is a good thing, unless she goes too far and deprives herself or her children. A woman who saves money responsibly transmits this value to her children. Her children learn to respect their father's possessions and to value his time, despite him giving freely of it. Women who spend wantonly disrespect men. Women who save wisely are highly valued members of society.

Women have different considerations than men early on the dating process. Women do well to get the following questions answered:

What is this man's quality as a provider?

Women need resources. A woman needs to know a man's prospects before she commits to him. This is not to say that every woman should expect to be with a millionaire. There are not a lot of them to go around! Rather, a woman needs a sober assessment of her own sexual market value, the number of children she would like to have, and clear expectations on what kind of providers are available to her. Despite the rampant propaganda to the contrary, barring major medical problems, children are not that expensive to raise well. Children need adequate food, shelter, and clothing for the duration of their childhoods. Beyond that, peaceful parenting is sufficient enough to ensure the child will have a happy, prosperous, and virtuous childhood. Nor should women automatically choose a lower provider because of the nobility of peaceful parenting. Moneymaking, for a man, is a personal growth project since a man pits himself against competitors in the marketplace. A man of low horizons may be the most peaceful dad, and for some women that is enough, a sandy shore just to be lucky to land on – but for some women, whose parents did better and thus she brings more to the table as a wife, this will not be sufficient. Peaceful parenting is largely the negation of negatives in common parenting strategies but this book will go above and beyond this at times in order to discuss *value added*. At a baseline, the world needs immoral parenting to stop. We often feel more motivated to desist from wrongdoing if we know the potentials that exist in the absence of immoral parenting.

A woman does well to look for a man who keeps a consistent sleep routine, is engaged in adding value to the lives of other men in an ethical manner, refrains from substance abuse, looks for opportunities to advance in the enterprise, is gainfully employed on principle, stays out of consumer debt, and pays his bills on time. Also, a woman needs a man who can save money, invest somewhat competently, potentially has family business connections, and can weather periods of personal financial austerity without stressing out too much. Personality is infectious and a stressy man will put undue stress on a woman that she does not need as she is juggling the responsibilities of childrearing and being a homemaker.

What about his moral quality?

What a man professes to be his values is not necessarily what is consistent with his behavior. Men have more moral agency than women because they are more capable of deciding and guiding society. As such, a woman will need to take a good look at what her prospective husband is "made of". Is he made of the right stuff? Is he kind of a scoundrel sometimes? Does he suffer from some kind of inborn insecurity? Is he morally excellent now or a prospect for later? Is he a loser? Is he a perpetual "project"?

Honesty is the defining feature of successful marriages. Lies introduce chaos, distrust, and inconsistency into a marriage. These eventually unravel the marriage and divorce is the nail in the coffin. Spouses should be honest with each other. They should discuss their childhoods with one another in a way that is respectful, curious, and measured. Over time, as they gain insights on one another, they serve to help each other out of whatever burdens they were carrying from their childhoods and into a life of volition and eventually (if they do it right), serenity.

A woman should look for a man who is honest with other men. He is transparent in his business dealings, sincere with his friends, the leader or near-leader of his family system (depending on his birth order and personal competence compared to his brothers), and is willing to work through the difficult truth he learns about himself during prayer or self-reflection. A man of moral fiber, of moral courage, is a man who can guide a family through its development and ensure the children reach adulthood in full grasp of their faculties. Stubborn, moral obstinance on the part of the man will limit the family's potential. Women who were raised well had courageous fathers themselves and will be well-suited to spot moral weakness in men. Is he given to self-indulgence? Is he a habitual masturbator? Does he skip from job to job without raising his earnings? Does he get into petty fights with others? Is he snobbish and preening? Is he socially isolated? These are all indicators of a tendency to "crumble" later on in the relationship. Weak men eventually give in to their women's shadows. In their existential need for comfort, which comes from not being able to face difficult moral questions in themselves and in the world, men become toxically feminine as they age and their testosterone levels drop. This tendency is only countered by self-knowledge and by a man surrounding himself with competent, courageous men as he ages. A woman needs to be on the lookout for moral weakness in a man because it will turn into treachery as he ages and becomes more and more unable to face the truth about himself. Women need to understand about themselves that their primary role in the family is to nurture. The man will abuse this natural tendency in the woman, if he is of low moral character. This leads to tremendous dissatisfaction and eventually, mutual self-deception. A woman cannot easily correct a man's overdependence on her as he ages and so she must be judicious in her choosing from the outset. A weak man will smother a good woman and debase her feminine dignity.

What is this man's relationship to risk?

Men tend to grow in relation to their risk tolerance. A man who takes greater risks tends to get greater rewards. Women are not natural risk takers. If a woman wants to ensure her family's social standing will improve over time, which is a far better ambition to have than to aspire for a career, she will need to reflect early on in the courtship whether the man has it in him to gradually take greater risks as he ages. A lay-about now will be a lay-about later. A go-getter now will likely be a go-getter later.

A woman needs to be on the lookout for healthy testosterone levels in a man. Testosterone helps a man tolerate risk. It gives him natural ease in the realm of achievement and around other men. Burly men have always done better than fay men, and they always will. Upper body strength is an indicator of testosterone. Physiognomy is very real and has never been debunked, despite what leftists say.

Will he protect me and our future children?

As government tax revenues continue to plummet, austerity measures are increased, mass migration's consequences are realized, and whites face a demographic cliff in the West, home and business security will drift further and further out of the hands of government police forces and into the hands of private entities. Men need men more than ever. Men are forming collective defense associations. The earliest vestiges of this have been in the form of the modern militia movement but collective defense associations will only go more mainstream. They will gain more mainstream appeal. Before the giant welfare programs of the 20th century, it was common for a man to belong to a fraternal organization. These were like unions where you paid your dues, gained employment opportunities, had access to affordable healthcare, and so forth. These organizations are going to make a strident return. A woman needs to look for a man who is forming the right bonds with his fellow men.

A man who protects his children is a man who has access to social and fiscal resources *and* has the right attitude about his family's future. Is he watchful and assertive or media-drunk and sarcastic? Are there layers of trust to him or does he belly-up and give everything away the moment there's undue pressure in his environment? Is he a predator or prey? There is a constant war in society between fabulously wealthy psychopaths and the middle class. Is this man aware of the stakes, as I laid them out in *Dead West Walking* and *Rise And Fight*, or is he a useful rube for the banking class? What is his relationship to firearms? Does he keep himself athletic and dangerous or sedate and masturbatory? These assessments matter. A strong man will not blink under such scrutiny. He will be glad for the scrutiny. A weak man will evade these questions or denigrate them for whatever reason.

Men and women need to be in fundamental agreement on their values, if they are going to get along for the rest of their lives. They need to have similar values on money, parenting philosophy, conflict resolution, religion, and family roles. I have not yet given a treatment to conflict resolution, so let us have a look.

Conflict is a part of the early going in a marriage, given that most people come into marriages with problems. How a husband and wife resolve conflict becomes how the children resolve conflict, so it is a notable case of "ounce of prevention, pound of cure" to be able to square up on sound principles that keep conflict from escalating. Conflict is an opportunity to learn. Conflict is almost always a power struggle. Usually it is the woman who is not willing to live or die by her husband's judgment that is the source of a power struggle. This, of course, means that a man has a responsibility to be of sound judgment. My books, livestreams, and recordings serve as tools and lessons to improve men's judgment. When men have sound judgment, women can leave the broader social world of conceptual wrangling and hone in on the home – where they shine. This is a critical delineation of roles and responsibilities that practically no one in the world is articulating to this degree. When a woman marries a man, she passes from the care of her father into the care of her husband. Women will always be dependent upon men in a way that men will not be dependent on women. As such, the man and woman in difficult or uncomfortable times must default to the man's judgment to guide them through. This is no trifle for the man, though some treat it this way and develop into scoundrels or tyrants over time. They become private torturers in their hidden family nests. This is wrong. A man, in his dealings and in his judgment, must remain as upright as if all the spousal power struggles that crop up in his marriage had to be resolved publicly in front of an audience of a thousand kings. Only through the man's accountability to universal truth and moral virtue can conflict resolution take place. If the man strays, a woman is *hard pressed* to right the ship. Women are not natural arbiters of conflict, despite their prevailing presence as judges in the world's modern court systems. The highest authority in any social system will be a man or the system has gone rotten at some point. This is true from a single family all the way up to a nation of people.

A man bears primary responsibility for any conflict because he is the natural leader of the family. Feminism tries to take advantage of this fact by inciting women to kick up a fuss anytime their impulses are not satisfied. A man has no need to satisfy the impulses of a woman. She may have impulses and demands but *any* conflict, when *slowed down* enough, will allow a man to see where he has been unwise. Perhaps he chose a woman that would not healthily detach from her family of origin in order to attach to him in a timely manner. Perhaps he chose a woman with a high body count who has secret, private fantasies in moments of weakness about the men she has permitted inside of her. Perhaps he chose a "high maintenance" woman, a woman who lacks a rich inner life. When the conflict is slowed down, the man can then inquire into the nature of the power struggle and understand what insecurities in the woman are driving her to misbehave. Of course, the man *must* be willing to hold himself to the same standard. He must address his own insecurities so that he does not stray from the marriage or punish the woman. A man must be a benevolent leader, not a feminist "co-equal" or an impatient aggressor. He must lead through goodness and kindness, even when a woman is *really* pressing his buttons. Those buttons were put there by his own parents, not by the wife. A man must not deride a woman and hurt her self-worth. But neither should he simp for her and idealize her for her vanity's sake. She is good or he chose poorly. Same goes for a woman: either her man is good or she and her father failed to accept the advances of a good man.

When we have the fundamental belief that our spouse is good, we will weather the voices of doubt that lie to us or try to build the case that the other person *changed*. People do not change unless they are seduced by substances and outside influences. Why would a husband ever permit this to happen? Why would a man allow his woman to have "male friends"? Why would a man allow his wife to follow a bunch of sexy man-boys on social media? Why would a man allow his wife to be indoctrinated by reality TV or lifestyle blogs? Why would a man indulge substance abuse in his wife? Why would a man himself do the male version of any of these? Only because he is weak and cannot further integrate into the fraternal order. Men and women need to be independently committed to goodness so that they are married in truth. If a person is good in their identity, all issues, conflicts, troubles, and stresses become opportunities to grow and improve morally. Feelings of abandonment and rupturing distress become attributable to the *past*, not to the spouse.

Let us go through some of the most common conflicts in marriage and how these principles and observations apply.

Fighting About Money

Couples[57] fight about money when there is not clarity on finances and especially when a woman has a career. A woman places herself into the role of a man when she has a career and especially when she out earns a man, which puts stress on the marriage as the man is supposed to be the main provider. The man who controls the family's finances spares his family one of the main family stressors in the modern era. Men must take it upon themselves as early as possible in their adulthoods to build their finances, build their skills, and learning how to live within a budget. The man must set up the budget and be rigid about it. The woman must learn to be creative with the budget. People have to live within their means, despite the abundance of consumer credit. Consumer credit benefits the elite banking class and has a similarly caustic effect on the family as pornography does, only worse because of its widespread social acceptance. A woman leaves the provision of her father and enters into the provision of her husband. She must accept this transition and not

---

[57] I do not like this word but we are using it for convenience's sake.

place onto her husband the earnings expectations of a man who has thirty years more of marketplace experience.

"The budget" sets the limits on the money relationship. A man does not need to be financially transparent with a woman but he *does* need to balance his risk-taking with familial considerations. He must remain committed to the basic physical needs of the children and wife: adequate food, shelter, and housing. There will be lean years. There may even be bankrupt years. But there should be enough. And it does not take *that much* to keep a family happy, so long as honesty and virtue are the currencies the family deals in. Women who are used to gilded, silver-spoon lifestyles must choose high earners and then respect the budget. You pay to play. Some men are going to go broke. That is the game. Family divorce courts give greedy women a way out of the game but the world will not be run by rapacious cat lady liberal judges for much longer. And greedy women are getting left behind because young men are in revolt, as they should be.

There are no "Joneses" to keep up with, despite people's media programming. Peaceful parents have no use at all for affluence-signaling. That which matters in this life is the truth, not material envy. Two hundred years ago, people were happy just to not have all the teeth in their mouths not fall out. A hundred and fifty years ago, people were just happy to have something to wipe their butts with other than rags. Most of the developing world in the past thirty years saw its first generation of car drivers out on the road. What matters is that we are healthy, we can further virtue in the world, and that we remain true. The latest gadget does not matter, on a personal level. We may need product innovation for business purposes and to make our homes more efficient or beautiful. This being said, most people are somewhat involved in "keeping up with the Joneses" and they get *results* this way. The whole Rich Housewives and HGTV subcultures *make people money.* We need to understand that a game is being played, not that this is what truly matters. When we can make that distinction to ourselves and our identities are rooted in virtue, we can make money decisions around the house in an enterprising manner – as opposed to a personal and emotional manner.

The budget is a force that works against acquisitive and covetous habits. When a man and woman can satisfy themselves to live within their means, or within certain bounds, the strain that money needs can have on a marriage is lessened. The budget is a kind of third-party appeal to any disagreements that arise. "Is this in the budget?" is the most basic appeal. When we have a healthy sense of limits, we regard our situation with the kind of humility that allows us to make sober, accurate improvements. One of the best ways to make more money is to live within our means. This teaches us the true nature of our earning potential and inspires us to become more efficient and effective. Easy credit perverts this basic growth process and has all manner of negative interpersonal consequences.

How To Deal With A Challenging Child

Every child is unique in their emotional needs. Some babies are "easy babies". Some cry, fuss, and demand a lot. This does not necessarily change as kids age. Some are just highly sensitive. They are more passionate than others. Parents often clash on how to parent these kids. A passionate, highly sensitive child can provoke intense feelings in one parent or the other. Peaceful parenting prevents all the endless squabbles and frustrations that come out of parents being at odds with one another on how to handle a challenging child. We reason and negotiate with children, that is the bottom line. We will discuss this point further in an upcoming section on spending individual time with each child you have.

Religion

Religion is one of the trickier points of disagreement to navigate between a man and woman. Whether a person of Western origin is connected to Christ or not is indicative of the quality of attachment they had to their parents and their parents to the grandparents. Atheism in today's age is an indication of low-quality attachment experienced in childhood.

The best way to heal religious division is for people to marry within their religious communities, for the titanic government program of mass migration to end, for the military industrial complex to stop subsidizing conflict in the Middle East, and for people to focus on honesty as the basis for their bonds. We can heal insecure attachment experienced in childhood through self-reflection. This allows us, in adulthood, to experience the religious element of our humanity in a way that is sincere.

Atheism is not a community. Rational atheism is not a community but a fad. Even the strongest, most rationally minded atheists demonstrably fall short on living up to the teachings of Christ. Atheists have interpersonal trust problems that they obfuscate with conceptual, intellectual arguments that attempt to shift the burden of proof onto believers – meanwhile dismissing the testament of their fellow man as inadmissible. If the pairing arises, a Christian spouse has the responsibility to bring their atheist spouse into communion, however gradually, with their fellow man. Love wounds from childhood run deep and we must be patient with people as they learn to trust at the most fundamental levels. Christians are right to say a prayer for non-believers.

Extended Family Issues

"The in-laws" is a common source of anguish for married couples. Invasive extended family members only cause trouble when they are emotionally immature. Emotionally mature extended family members give support in the right ways and do not behave in an invasive or distant manner. Immature extended family weigh in when their opinion is not sought or is of low value, cross boundaries in a habitual manner, drag people into their own problems, project their insecurities onto the spouse that does not belong to their family, and contribute all sorts of other complications and maladies to the social milieu.

Parents of peacefully parented children need to provide their children with a united front toward outsiders, no matter how well they mean. Peaceful parents, when it is applicable, need to disseminate the emotional information provided by extended family members to their children in a way that makes sense. Not everyone is going to buy in on peaceful parenting but this is not automatic grounds for cutting people out of one's life. This is a tricky balance because children should never be exposed to abuse and adults can have adult relationships where one's children are not involved. Some people warm up to peaceful parenting over time and can be gradually introduced to the children, if enough goodwill is there. Some people never do but they are not overt abusers and can be around kids a bit without troubles.

With peaceful parenting, we cannot spare our children from ever being hurt, lied to, or rudely tricked by people out in the world. We do not do these things to them ourselves because when trouble comes their way from people out in the world, they will not speak the language of abuse. They will not fall into the role of victim because of prior conditioning. Children will naturally become curious about extended family members, especially when they become teenagers, and may want to meet some of these people for their own insight and learning. Barring situations where extended family is litigious or invasive, our children benefit from us fostering their learning processes and encouraging them toward others – even if there is a bit of "rough stuff". Peaceful parenting is not "isolationist", as liberal cowards in the media often term people like Ron Paul or Donald Trump, but it is measured, reasoned preparation in anticipation of irrational, unreasonable people and cultures out in the world. Who better to help our children deal with "rough stuff" in the world than us? This does not mean "toughening up" our children, in the classical sense, but it does mean helping them to gradually build social resilience in a way that is not overwhelming to them.

Grandparents who did not peacefully parent themselves are in the learner's seat for any contributions they have to a grandchild who is being peacefully parented. Grandparents have lots of experience in what *not* to do, but rarely are they the set of parents that chose to end the intergenerational cycle of abuse. Where grandparents did well, they have insights to offer but they also need to have the humility to admit their faults and limit themselves when they are out of their depth. The promise lies with the younger generations and grandparents need to regain their sense of curiosity in order to maintain their relevance as caretakers.

Extended family is an important but lost institution in America. It has to be rebuilt on honest principles, not just for convenience's sake. Peaceful parenting is not about obligating yourself to spend time with people who are not interested in you.

Distant Husbands

Men can become distant from their wives for a number of reasons. Most commonly it is because of working long hours or from tiring of female nagging, which we will cover soon. Distancing is a common coping mechanism for men because historically, men needed to stay engaged with their working lives in order to provide for their families. Men tend to push things under and keep going on. We live in a "socially distanced" age of socialist bureaucracy, which solely exists at the expense of family, community, and religious networks. Men also distance themselves from their wives because they do not know how to troubleshoot, negotiate, maintain their patience, or express themselves within the marriage, though these circumstances are less common than leftists would have us believe.

Men need to remember that they are needed and valued by their family. Their personal presence greatly benefits everyone in the family. Women need to remember to entice their husbands toward them by not putting on weight, staying reasonably shapely, cooking quality meals, keeping a tidy home, and not dealing with the children in the way men deal with their children.

Distant fathers run the risk of their sons becoming homosexuals or even transsexuals. Both categories have markedly increased mental illness rates and 40% of transsexuals attempt to commit suicide, which is nine times the rate of the normal population[58]. Mothers exacerbate paternal distancing by coddling their sons and reducing their exposure to healthy male adults in the community. Mothers unable to express their frustration with paternal distancing or to entice their husbands back to the home will put their frustrations onto their sons, oftentimes, and the result is a son who is doubly resentful toward the father – both from his own lack and from his mother's lack.

Some men become emotionally distanced from their families because they go through a crisis where they think they could have done better for themselves. They project the knowledge they have now into their past selves and give in to fantasies of a better life. This can become destructive, instead of instructive, if the man decides the woman or the children are the cause of his dissatisfaction. These men need to understand that men *do* get better as they age. They become better providers. They gain insights and experience. They *would* have made better decisions, once upon a time, but life is imperfect. Our knowledge of the ideal is what allows us to make our lives better *now*, not in some fantasy life that exists only if we detonate our relationships. Men, in the age of pornography, especially get caught up on the, "I could have had a

---

[58] https://news.yahoo.com/she-really-warrior-transgender-migrant-120035145.html

more physically attractive woman" longing. Women do not get prettier as they age. Their physical attractiveness peaks somewhere in their mid-20's. Men continue to get more handsome into their mid to late 40's, granted they keep in good shape and eat healthy diets. The wives of successful men have to, to some degree, fend off advances from younger women who see what the man has brought to fruition. This is all made easier when the man realizes that trust and your reputation *with yourself* counts for a lot. Sure, powerful men can bounce around between wives but they lose esteem with themselves every time they bounce. There is a significant cost to tasting the forbidden fruit. Marriage is a lifetime vow. Even more so than failing to fulfill a business contract, the downsides of failing the marriage contract can lead to decrepitude in old age – not to mention the catastrophic consequences of divorce on a man's children. The men most concerned with a woman's appearance, beyond her maintaining her body's ideal weight and dressing nicely, are men that are just *too* into women. A man who is adding to the world's virtue does not sit back and compare his woman to models and pornographic whores. If he is, for some reason, it is because he is compensating for some lack of inner worth.

Nagging Wives

Nagging is a form of verbal abuse. A woman who nags is a woman who engages in persistent faultfinding, complaints, or demands. This is the main social currency of women who are not self-knowledgeable. The voting franchise for women and the modern welfare state exist because propertied men, no so long ago, buckled under the weight of female nagging. Women have been entitled to believe that they can verbally accost men without facing retaliation or consequences of any kind. The average liberal woman believes that any terseness or outward expression of annoyance in her direction after her nagging is a form of abuse and "patriarchy". This is untrue because it was the nagging woman who initiated the aggression.

Men in the West have largely proven incapable of containing and reversing female nagging. This is partly because men have turned away from Christianity, which provided valuable lessons on dealing with female evil, but also because the industrial and post-industrial consumer age has changed women. Women used to see childrearing in terms of life and death stakes. Now, women see childrearing, at best, as an opportunity to foster the right "lifestyles" in their children. The death of cottage industries and the rise of the managerial state has meant that men have been pulled from the home. Men no longer check the mothering habits of women and have less of an effect on its guiding ethos. Women, when they were children growing up, took on vague feminist notions about parenting and have passed it on to the next generation. Male victims of female nagging had nags as mothers. Nagging is so pervasive that American culture is practically dead. There exist exceedingly few men, like Donald Trump or Mike Pence, who can contain and reverse female nagging in a competent manner.

Nagging is handled by never taking the bait with a woman. Mike Pence's debate performance against Kamala Harris serves as a near-perfect example.[59] A woman's pretty insults, digs, and complaints matter not. Our forefathers spent tremendous sweat and blood to entrust to us the machinery of civilization. When a man can be connected to his forefathers, he finds the will to silence female nagging. Since women who nag have engaged in verbal aggression, it is appropriate to silence, critique, insult, cajole, or neg a woman – but only in self-defense or in third party self-defense. Men who put their personal revenge fantasies, that they harbored toward their own mothers, into their self-defense eventually lose control of the situation by overplaying their hands. A man chooses the women around him, unless they are politicians and bureaucrats who rule him from above. Since a man chooses the women in

---

[59] Go look it up!

his personal life, he cannot reasonably exact punishment or revenge on them. He was the one that chose them. A man chooses, as an adult, whether he will continue to have a relationship with his mother, sister, cousin, or aunt. There is no room for nags in a man's adult life and any nagging experienced in boyhood can be remediated by moral confrontation or conscious estrangement as an adult.

Nagging women have extreme amounts of power because they have entrenched themselves in the bureaucracies of the family courts, the social work field, the public schools, and now into national politics. The "fiercest" female leaders in America, such as Nikki Haley, Megyn Kelly, Ellen DeGeneres, Ilhan Omar, or you name them, are notorious and obvious nags. Women do not achieve political dominion over men through competence and leadership but through verbal manipulation and nagging. It is not morally correct for a woman to hold executive leadership because there will always be a man more competent or deserving than her who has been gatekept because of feminism and the simping of weaker men. We live in a dominion of nagging women who have not been contained. This is sure to change in the coming decades.

The first step to deescalating female nagging in a marriage is to not marry a nagging woman like one's life depended on it, cause it almost always does. Absent that, it is important to define nagging and then to identify it every time it happens. A man, in his courtship with a woman, can help a woman to see her nagging and to understand its deleterious effects. He can help a woman to understand just *why* nagging is so commonly accepted today and why it is not going to go away anytime soon. She is going to get a lot of narcissistic supply in being a nag. She can nag her way to the top! But it will come at the price of peace and any semblance of male efficacy in the men in her personal life. The media promotes men who are fops and have been railroaded by female nagging as the ideal. She will get for herself all the trappings that evil can afford. But she will not keep her husband's respect or her children's adoration.

Just as men need to step away from philandering, so do women need to step away from nagging. Cheating is the man's "nuclear option" and nagging is the woman's. Both break the foundations of the marriage, one through a sudden crack and the other through a thousand small cracks. Female nagging is one of the primary contributors to male cheating, as men feel trapped by the mounds of verbal abuse and seek escape in the arms of a younger, demurer woman.

Nagging teaches children that you verbally abuse others to get what you want. It teaches children to develop elaborate, dissociative justifications for getting what they want, instead of being plainspoken and sincere. Male abusiveness has been overhyped by the media. There is no justification for nagging.

Family Stress

Parenting is an energy and sleep consuming task. Children are learning how to sleep consistently. Children are rambunctious and demanding. The house becomes untidy. Chores get missed. Bills are sometimes left forgotten. Appointments pepper the family's schedule. Things can meander toward the chaotic. Parents can feel "off center" and their stress piles up. This can lead to bickering, the "I can't hear you" game of hollering from one room to another at one another, and frustrations aplenty. It is important that families have a recuperation ritual built into every week or even every day. For most, prayer and going to church suffice. For parents who are lower intelligence or who tend to get easily overwhelmed, a daily meeting may be necessary. Going outside as a family is a major American ritual, especially for Americans who can trace their roots further back into American history. Going outside allows the family to step out of the family stress built up into the home, experience different stimulus, get some sunshine and fresh air, and spend time without the usual stimulation of electronic devices.

The husband and wife caught up in family stress can lose their personal autonomy and feel beholden at all times to the children's needs. Most parenting books teach parents to take a little "me time", which is incorrect. Peaceful parenting, and this book specifically as there will eventually be pale imitations, shows parents how to fully meet the needs of children so that family stress is largely prevented and one's responsibilities stay at a manageable level at all times. It is impossible to not have family stress of some kind with both parents working full time. A mother full time in the home for the children's main development up to the age of reason and then *perhaps* in the family business through the rest of their childhoods is ideal. Children have more needs and are a greater responsibility than conventional parenting books written by research-based liberal women with PhD's let on. Most of these books are aimed at the basics: stopping the spanking, using Alfred Adler's "positive discipline", and getting the kids into college. Boring! This book is way cooler than those books.

Men have ultimate agency when it comes to resolving conflicts. All of the major stress points in marital conflict are avoided when the man knows what he is getting into with a woman, avoids red flags on her part, and then remains engaged and committed through the courtship and into marriage as a judicious, self-reflective, negotiating, and ultimately, moral force in the marriage. If he can avoid the Boomer Libertarian approach to interpersonal relationships, he has a chance to help his woman grow into a splendid mother who runs the home like a champion. This becomes a great source of pride and daily pleasure for both the man and woman. A man is responsible for the condition of his family more so than the woman because men have more agency than women. Women have lower boundaries, are more impressionable and malleable, and ultimately have different evolutionary incentives.

Men need to choose relatively untroubled women who can be rehabilitated from liberalism or who are natural conservatives waiting for the man's "finishing touches." Men need to choose like their future children have a vote. A man needs to weigh his own vote against the vote of five or more children that he can reasonably deduce will be clearer in their thinking than him and less traumatized than he is. Will she make a blue-chip mother? If there was a fair for good mothering, would she win a blue ribbon for her maternal instincts? For being the best at vacuum cleaning, reading storybooks, or making due within a budget? Will she be the sweetest? This is how a man needs to conceptualize his choice. Far too many men are socially isolated and they forget their will be a future audience for their decisions, even if he absconds with her to a mountaintop and never lets her out of what used to be a grizzly bear's den. We are interconnected and our social decisions reverberate out.

Women need to choose men who are tough enough to face down the waves of dysgenic breeding that have happened because of the major welfare states of the West. Women have been picking "bad boys", because of state intervention, and they are selecting for aggression because everyone is anticipating major wars in the wake of empire collapse. Women should not be choosing soy boys, Third World thugs, bearded gaping mouth gamer boys, unfeeling corporate cogs, or dumb idiots, if possible. Women should be trying to find First World, loving, strong men with some zest – men who can work through their own autism and contribute to an ever-greater degree to the grand experiment of Western Civilization. Let's face it, ladies, you are going to want to find men who read books like this one and who can bring in a steady income. Drop me an email if you are in the middle of your search. I can help! Barbaric apes may seem enticing in the short run but they always turn into child abusers and sometimes even child molesters – that is if they are even around later on. The most heated and media-celebrated cultures are barbaric rape cultures but these are not the kinds of cultures that will produce functional, upstanding men.

Spousal Bonding

We want peaceful parents to be in-love with one another. We want them to find the most enjoyment possible that this life has to offer. This enriches their union and puts a *glow* on peaceful parenting for the kids. When two good people, a man and a woman, come together in marriage, there are a number of things they can do to keep the flame alive and well. Here just before we get on to a full picture of what peaceful parenting is, we will discuss five ways that parents can keep a healthy and hardy attachment:

1) Keep up the contact: Men and women alike benefit from holding eye contact, cuddling from time to time, wrestling or tickling, back scratches and massages, hugs, kisses on the lips (preferably when the children are not around as they learn this behavior and try it on others and others often come from sexually abused backgrounds), holding hands, and doing chores together – especially outdoor ones like raking leaves or feeding livestock. Men do well to give their wives a pat on the butt from time to time. Women do well to rub their men's feet when they get home or to kiss their man on the cheek. Physical contact increases the production of oxytocin, the "bonding hormone". Married people need to use contact to maintain their bond.

2) Have honest conversations and do stuff together: When people have dealt with their traumas sufficiently, their marital conversations have a lot to do with aging, with articulating aspects of their personality that they could not before, the kids and extended family, and active interests cultivated in adulthood. Men and women have different fields of interest in mature, adult roles. There is a natural give and take reciprocity to supporting these interests in one's spouse. We do not expect married couples to go on

fishing or hunting trips together, unless they are living off-grid away from modernity or they are retired, but sometimes people have these shared interests and we celebrate their ability to connect. Sometimes married couples exercise together. This does not give a green light to the woman to start grunting and putting on *beef* on her haunches, but it does mean that exercise can help a man be more of a man and a woman maintain more of a womanly figure. Couples who have honest conversations will honor their individual differences but still find common ground and activities that help each achieve their potential. Some couples take up dancing. The man sometimes lifts the woman a bit or twirls her about. They are both dancing but in the art there is a distinction between them that allows them to be more self-expressed.

People are *wed in truth*. This means that a man and woman form a marriage union as a commitment to keeping each other honest. This does not mean some kind of active meddling on one another's part.

Honest conversations sometimes involve an examination of personal feelings toward one another. It is important to differentiate between unfulfilled feelings from childhood and adult, empirical observations that inform one's *adult feelings*. Many couples fall into "honest communication" traps where this distinction is not made. This turns into co-therapy, which is inappropriate to courtship and marriage and is largely a liberal 20th century invention, and the couple never achieves existential maturity. We are not here to directly heal our spouse's wounded inner child but we can offer support and listening, so long as the balance of the relationship is respected.

Honesty has a lot to do with co-creating. This means that we collaborate to do our daily good work so that we can remain connected to our artistic and creative selves. Then we fashion a grand, beautiful existence where our artistic visions are realized. Our artistry is inseparable from our values. As collaborative creators, we discuss our insights, inspirations, intrigues, and enjoyments in a confident way. When we stew in this kind of creative environment, we help each other to make our dreams come true. Marriage does not have to feel like a prison, a dragging obligation, a mutual deception, or a showpiece for the social approval of others (usually on Facebook or Instagram). With honest conversations we can directly engage the genius of our spouse and leave pretenses and postures behind. Couples can only get to this level of fulfillment if they respect the natural roles, red flags, sources of conflict, and essential foundations laid down earlier in this chapter.

3) Do favors for one another and help each other out: Men need things done around the house and they will ask their women to do this or that, for the efficient upkeep of the home. Men need help with heavy lifting, they concern themselves with spot childcare in moments where the woman's tasks require two hands, sometimes both need to handle a farm or gardening chore together, or a pressing errand needs to be run. Couples need to remain conscious that there is a balance in the relationship. Favors and help need to be reciprocal, within the bounds of appropriate roles, and need to be recognized consistently with gratitude. This fosters that environment of co-creation and collaboration that bonds a couple in virtue and purpose. Chores, errands, and mutual help are an opportunity to "pay a deposit" into the goodwill of the relationship. However,

this is not cause for the "you owe me" game. Rather than a selfish, "you owe me" approach to correcting an imbalance in the reciprocity, each person needs to remember to remain committed to the higher purpose of the marriage: to raise children and to honor God. We are simply keeping each other honest to *the truth*, not getting lost in favor-tracking. When we know that our spouse is fundamentally good, we know that they will autonomously tend to the balance of the relationship just like we will. We are both contributing and seeking to improve. Our gratitude helps us to realize every day that something wonderful is being built over the decades. We will age together in grace because we each sought to be better according to an outside standard of excellence, not each other's temporary, passing needs.

4) Give each other gifts: Some people like gifts. Gift giving is not for everyone. Gifts should never be used to manage someone's greed or anxiety. Some people have a hole in their hearts that they need filled with material acquisitions. Or they have fears about the relationship they put into gift form. This character issue needs to be addressed in the courtship through conscious dialogue, not well into marriage. For people who are not covetous, gifts can be a source of delight and gratitude. Men can give their wives a nice bracelet or necklace, a leather-bound Bible, a large framed photo of the family, a massage from a masseuse, an hour or a day at the spa, a delicious dark chocolate, a love note, flowers (which are universally loved by all well-adjusted women), or a car. Gifts should be given in service of the marriage's purpose, not for temporary bumps of excitement and sex that relieve tension in the home. Tension should be resolved the same way family stress is resolved.

Women can give their husbands what their allowance or side gig permits. Healthy men have little need for gifts from women. A woman can give her man a small gift on Christmas, a handmade blanket or scarf in the winter time, a sweet note on the bathroom mirror from time to time, or a tool he has been needing for a job around the place. The truth is that a woman gives man the greatest gifts there are: children, homecooked meals, and a nice den for nightly sleep. Women give every day with their homemaking, especially in an age where they could run out the door and get easy promotions and international banker money for pursuing careers as feminists. Mind you, there are outliers, women who are exceptionally intelligent compared to other women (who cluster in the center of the bell curve) who will just bump into piles of cash through actual genius. These women should not be discouraged from participating in the economy, with the big caveat that they "pay it forward" by having children above replacement level themselves. The empirical fact is that they are far fewer and farther between than the media has brainwashed everyone to believe. A few women out there give gifts by making everyone rich but these are not women who benefited from grift, such as degrees, preferential hiring, and ideological sermons at "team meetings." These women tend to be discreetly nestled in family businesses, fighting as immigration patriots a la Phyllis Schlafly, or as undeniable talents in finance. These women are bound by the same civilization-making ethos of putting family first as any other woman is.

5) Vacationing: Vacations are the sweet repose for a married couple, if done right. Domestic vacations within the United States are preferable to international vacations, but vacations to Europe are also somewhat preferable –

especially over the Third World. Money is best spent domestically to add to the lives of one's countrymen. People should make a sincere attempt to spend their money with small business countrymen, first and foremost. Vacations offer the family time outside of the home that can be used for extra rest, relaxation, newfound adventures, and perspective on the home life itself. Vacations offer newfound sensations and stimulus that can inform the family of its purpose or simply help everyone to bask in the glow of the family's love. Vacations are a celebration of achievement, not a consumerist getaway where Mom and Dad secretly let out their worst sides while the kids are at the swimming pool. Some families find it particularly recharging to go to a cabin in the woods by a lake and enjoy the outdoors. Some families want an urban getaway where they can visit museums, sample fine restaurants, and be in the buzz. Every family has different tastes. It is just how personality works. Vacations can be a taste of the high life to motivate and inspire couples to keep going. When America had a robust middle class that was in charge of the government, vacationing was a common and enjoyable pastime for everyone. Vacations are a temporary improvement in material circumstances so that families can glimpse for themselves a life less than ordinary. There is no way to reproduce the culture of inspiration that comes from a vibrant, expansive middle class engaged in a vacation culture. Life is meant for savoring, not slaving.

Spousal bonding is an everyday kind of thing. This does not mean we should get down on ourselves if it does not happen that way. Sometimes men are called away from the home for days or weeks at a time. Sometimes there is not time for a phone call or things get rather busy. Spousal bonding may have to be as simple as putting on the wedding band in the morning. Peaceful parenting is not simply about not messing up our kids. It is about teaching our children to be in love with life so that they will live enchanted and fulfilling adulthoods. How are we going to achieve that if the main adult to adult relationship they are exposed to is one of apathy, avoidance, constant busyness, conflict, or annoyance? Couples need to be in consistent communication, always updating one another on the joy and wonder of raising children and living as healthy, meaning-making adults. Rituals give form to our enduring qualities and allow us to participate. The quality of our relationships is built *one interaction at a time*. We have the choice to build up a glistening mansion on the hill or a stinky hovel fit for pigs. This gets transmitted to our children and forms their expectations for what they will get later on. There is a great tally being kept, whether we admit it or not, and there are few second chances.

Chapter Five: Peaceful Parenting

This is not a specifically a child development book but we will be drawing from some of the early markers of development for a child in order to illustrate the principles of peaceful parenting at work.

Since we have defined what peaceful parenting is *not*, laid the foundation for parents coming together, discussed identity, and explored self-knowledge as the guiding foundation for peaceful parenting, let us get into what peaceful parenting *is*. As defined earlier, peaceful parenting is the commitment to reasoning with children through all stages of their development. You can begin to negotiate with children as they become more and more communicative. Communication begins with hunger and sleep and continues until the child is grown. Parents have a need to train the children for adulthood and children have a need to do whatever, whenever.

Early Experiences In Parenting Well

Mothers are the primary touchpoint for all early childhood negotiation. Negotiation begins with an assessment of needs. A mother needs sleep to function and a baby needs sleep on its own schedule. Mothers open up the primordial, ancient negotiation process that all peacefully parented children are instilled with by gently encouraging the child to fall asleep when night comes and by finding times in the day when the baby will fall asleep with some predictability. In the early going, there is little predictability and a lot of sleep deprivation. As the infant leaves the "fourth trimester" and comes into the mother's world of the home, the infant begins to find consonance with the mother's rhythms and patterns. The mother's encouragement and patience softens the disorientation of leaving the womb and processing the *separateness* of mother and child, mother and father, bed from bath, and so forth. Object permanence, realizing that objects in the environment exist whether the baby perceives them or not, begins around the age of eight months. The rudiments of a conceptual mind are formed for the baby. Hunger and sleepiness begin to be concepts the child can convey, usually through wining or crying, and sometimes through sign language if the parent chooses to train their child thusly.

Liberal parenting is modeled around permissiveness. This is to say that liberal parents *do know* what is good, what healthy standards are, but they deliberately choose to undermine healthy standards by "permitting" a child to break those standards. This permissiveness is then regarded as the model standard. Children do not come into the world in a perfectly civilized state. They are given to their impulses. They run around, scream as loudly as they can, and break things are part of the experimentation process. They fight against sleep. They much prefer eating sweets and carbs to anything else. Children are *unclear* on how organized society works. They need molding and encouragement toward ideal standards. Liberal parents signal that these standards mean less when they engage in permissiveness. Liberals do not believe in any hard and fast rules about the world, other than white people are racist and rich people only became rich through deception. Peaceful parents engage in far less permissiveness and as a result, lend more significance to the negotiation process. The equation that forms in a child's mind during their early years is not one of, "Yeah, but sometimes you give in to your impulses because that's *creative* and tasteful" but instead something more akin to, "I have animal instincts that I need to work to wed to my higher ideals." Permissiveness erodes agency and it masquerades as a practice in agency. Children will decide later on when to toy with standards, if they do at all. This is not a choice a parent makes on behalf of the child.

Larger negotiations around food and hunger begin as the child starts to differentiate foods and assert their preferences. Children *love* sugar. Sugar rots their teeth. Parents commonly use candies to get kids to eat the things the kids do not want to eat, such as spinach or beef. This shortcuts an essential negotiation process that needs to happen. If children learn, from the outset of their lives, that candy is the reward for doing difficult things that you do not want to do, they develop an unnecessary attachment to candy *and* the smarter ones figure out that you simply do the minimum necessary to get candy. Candy and gifts are not negotiating tools. They are deck-stacking devices for parents who lack the patience to sit with the time-consuming process of habituating their children to sometimes boring foods. Candy was a luxury in the pre-industrialized West, not so long ago. It was a rare luxury, not a daily bribery device. Parents' reliance on candy in the home is sign of parental fixation on sugar as a personal coping mechanism and a lack of emotional mastery. Children are not mentally capable of dealing with temporary energy bumps in their bodies that they later come down from but there their parents are, using candy for mood management in their children.

Children need a standard amount of protein, carbs, fat, and sodium in their diet. Incentivizing children to eat foods that they do not want to, using maybe a fruit or a vegetable they prefer here and there, is far preferable to using sugary treats. This often means that parents have to work to get sugar and processed foods out of their diets. That is an understandable and difficult process for some. The hard-won experience of overcoming these food fixations can be imparted to the child in a way that helps the child to be sugar resilient in later life. Same goes for if a parent has lost a lot of weight, beat a substance addiction, or recovered from a significant debt spiral. Our children *should* learn from our own life experiences but they should not be abandoned to flounder and drown in the problems that once plagued us.

Some children are easier. They *like* meat and veggies. You can get them to eat a chicken thigh by telling them they will get a grape tomato afterwards. Some children are challenging and willful, traits to be celebrated, and will seek to turn meal time into a drama. That is alright. We simply remember to be patient, reason with the child, and look to see if there are frustrations or imbalances developing outside of mealtime that are being expressed during mealtime. Everything in parenting is interconnected. There are no mysteries. A challenging child needs rigor, structure, attention, love, and cultivation. Same goes for an easier child. There may be a dynamic between them that we need to get curious about and attend to. We will get to sibling dynamics soon.

After the food negotiations are well underway, we arrive at potty training. There are whole tomes dedicated to potty training. To peacefully parent during potty training means to not use shame as a training tool. That is most people's fallback when they become overwhelmed by poop on the floor, rank smells emanating from half utilized diapers, undies being flushed down the toilet, urination spots on the underside of things we did not expect, and other highlights of potty training that trigger our disgust response. For children, pottying is not something to be ashamed of, spooked by at the potential of disgusting our parents, and *hiding* in the bathroom – despite our fears of the lights being out or the toilet making loud flushing sounds. Potty training is one of the first times a child gets to exercise some personal leadership. Parents learn to follow the child's lead for the first time. The child is taught the relevant facts, reminded of them with some regularity, and supported as he learns to endeavor to achieve. Parents who do not follow the child's lead on potty training end up feeling frustrated and their patience thins. Some children will potty train in a couple of weeks. Some children will take up to a year. Every child is on a different schedule.

The same goes for learning to read. Studies show that children learn to read in stages, at different rates and beginning at different ages, and that adult literacy is not impacted by children learning to read *earlier* than others. We have to afford ourselves the curiosity to see our child learn at different rates than their siblings and other children in the community. This does not mean that we sit back and become passive, telling ourselves they will get it when they get it. It means that we observe what their tendencies are, how they do, and calibrate ourselves accordingly. This is one of the fundamentals of being a good teacher. We draw from our repertoire as teachers in order to raise our children. Either we do or someone else will, so we may as well do it right and do it peacefully.

Peaceful parenting means having more than one child, if possible. The proverbial only-child misses out *dearly* on formative negotiating and bonding experiences that children in multiple-sibling households gain. Parents who can, within medical and biological reason, afford to have another child should have another child. We need conscientious people to breed. We are in a glut of work-averse, welfare-dependent people being raised as an echo of expanded welfare access during the Clinton, Bush, and Obama administrations. These people will have to be *won over* to peaceful parenting, if possible, whereas people who are peacefully parented from the get-go will be much more able to get up and get going with the business of making civilization run.

We have ground-setting work to do in anticipation of the birth of our second child. We need to be communicating to our first child that there will be a second child, that that is a *baby* in mom's belly, and we need to step up our *love resource* output when the second child comes. We need to "get in shape" emotionally for the second child. Some parents are blindsided when a second child comes and the first starts acting up because their sense of normalcy is disturbed. The first child is so special but we need to remember those wonderful feelings to be able to give them to the next child and the next child after that. Notching "one on the board" for the next generation is a deeply gratifying experience and our feelings of pride and wonder should not be denied to the next child. As for communicating with our first child that a second is coming, you can talk concepts over with babies. You can and should talk to your first when they are infants, or sooner. You want to habituate your child to a conversational relationship from the outset. Children have to go through a huge learning process to be able to communicate their internal needs, frustrations, wants, trepidations, etc. As much as possible, it is good to establish this dialogue before a second child is born. A second child has a huge impact on the first. We want to manage the transition with proactive communication and *credible* assurances that our firstborn will continue to get their love resources and their needs met.

With a second child we become mediators. Much of the early going is devoted to conflict around toys. The firstborn is used to playing with whatever toy, whenever. The second child simply grabs at whatever, whenever. With a patient hand, we have to ensure both children can have fun without pinning too much on any one toy. Parents make a critical mistake in this stage when they assign, in front of their first child, *special importance* on one toy or another. Out of their own insecurities, they jump the gun on nurturing positive identification between an object and their child's personality. "This is *your* special teddy bear I bought just for you," is roughly the line. New parents need to be aware that for a young toddler, this does not process. Toddlers do not need to be externalizing their sense of security onto toys they sometimes cannot control. Children do not need talismans. They need *internal* security via the mood management their parents have consciously fostered. Some parents will say, "Well, my kid just came up with their special teddy all on their own" to which this author responds, "Does one parent or the other have a special possession they are magnetized to? Or does one parent or the other use the child himself as a possession?" Toddlers need conceptual engagement, not grug brain pawing over physical items. Toddlers get to live at a conceptual level when their parents are engaging them with *meaning-making*, instead of, "Joe, stop fighting with your brother over the truck. You both get a turn!" The play itself is not, "I get this toy, you get that toy." The play itself is negotiation. Kids do not want to manipulate inanimate objects because that is what gives them kicks. They manipulate the objects in order to *learn* and see how the new information incorporates into their schematics for how the world operates. Some parents get caught up on appearances and lose their intellectual depth. They project this onto their children and sow the seeds of bickering and the "mine!" game.

Teaching kids about property rights happens as the child *separates* from the parent, starting around age five or six – when kids become markedly less cuddly and attached. The parent bears the ultimate responsibility of keeping out of the reach from the toddlers the toys that belong to the older children. The parent is a custodian of the learning process around property rights. When kids are toddlers, toys are presented and children play with them. Boys play with toys appropriate to boys. Girls play with toys appropriate to girls. Toys can be had for a dollar. Novel toys that two or more children are particularly drawn to and likely to fuss over ultimately belong to the parent and the parent needs to demonstrate that this is the parent's toy. Rather than, "Timmy! Damnit! Let your brother have a turn," parents need to *discuss* toys. Parenting involves so much talking. Talk with your kids about why the toy is preferred. Turn it into a tool for conceptualization and articulation. Get the children talking to each other. Get them negotiating about who prefers when to play with what. When children begin to separate and want their own rooms or own spaces, as most do, then it will be time for them to have bookcases, chests, desks, and armoires to keep their stuff in. The parent trains the kids to manage their growing assortment of individual possessions in a manner that does not overwhelm the child, as is evidenced by perpetual messes on the floor and untidy, unkempt rooms. When kids are toddlers, this is as basic as working with them to tidy up a playroom after the fun has been had. When they are a good deal older, this means helping them to prune the toys and items that have lost their allure or utility.

When children get to the age of reason, parents gradually give full possession to their children over toys, clothing, and later on, money and investments. As they are capable, and we find out by testing them and quizzing them, children need to be able to make the connection between their care or lack of care for a possession and preferable or not preferable outcomes. Some parents see this distinction come to the fore in the child's thinking and decide, "Hey, it's time for my child to own a pet!" After all, there *is* something adorable about children and young animals together. Parents need to be attentive here to understand when their children can start to take care of the needs of another creature altogether and when children will be more pressed in learning to take care of their *own* needs. Parents sometimes do not take into account that older children may already be taking it upon themselves to help out with the younger kids (though that is not their *expected* role as they did not have a choice over whether or not another sibling was born). "Too many pets syndrome" turns into a disaster and seems to be a uniquely suburban phenomenon. The last thing a kid needs is for a pet to die from neglect on their watch and a parent to say, "Well, you should have done better."

Children take a natural interest in the wellbeing of their siblings. This is only disrupted when parents are pitting children against each other, instead of training them to work in unison in the interests of virtue, Christ, family, sports and studies, business, nation, etc. Peaceful parents need to instill in their children a sense of belonging to the family, of collaboration and friendly competitiveness (without the "comparing game"), and of *help* instead of caretaking for one another. In some unfortunate families, a parent passes away or is maimed or enfeebled and is unable to fulfill their full responsibilities. In these families, an older child will have to look after their younger siblings. This is a lifeboat scenario that we pray visits as few families as possible. The standard operating procedure for intact, whole families is that older siblings help their younger siblings but do not have essential responsibilities pawned off onto them by inattentive parents. We want to encourage older siblings to help their younger siblings in the spirit of, "I did this myself only recently and can help you out". An older sister is not mama. An older brother is not papa. Kids should not have to play these roles. Siblings need mutual intimacy, to whatever degree each is capable, so that in adulthood they are bastions of sanity and utility to one another – not resentful, bitter adversaries who survived something together over a period of years, long ago. Just because a sibling was older and in a leader role in the childhood home does not mean that a younger child will be unable to supersede the older sibling later on when both are in the marketplace. Peaceful parents teach their children to value merit over arbitrary authority, like age and size. Peaceful parents do not lead simply because they are biological adults. They lead because they are *capable* parents. They need to teach the art of *capable living* to their children. When children understand that they do best when they have one another's best interests at heart, just like the "seeing each other as fundamentally *good*" piece I was talking about with spousal conflict resolution earlier, children will bond over how they enrich each other's lives. Petty squabbling will feel like a distant figment of some earlier era of society.

Peaceful parenting is not some complex science where we are required to be up to date on all the latest scientific journals and looking over our shoulders at all times for our faults. You reason through everything. Reasoning may be exhausting for you. It is a muscle. The earlier you commit yourself to being self-knowledgeable, the easier peaceful parenting will come to you.

Articulation: A Parenting Superpower

We have established that children are meaning-making creatures. Everywhere they go, they get *into* whatever is going on. They are drawn to novelty and incorporate new experiences with their pre-existing schemas. One of the failures of Golden, Silent, Boomer, and Gen X generation parenting is that children were placed in front of TVs to consume unending liberal programming, which has placed a high value on social justice and globalizing nativist sentiment out of people – not exactly the most rigorous ideas to be inculcated with. To peacefully parent, we need to spare our children the propaganda but also make them resilient for the adult challenges that lie ahead.

Aside from imparting a logically consistent set of values to our children, we can work with them to articulate meaning. In practical terms, this looks a lot like explaining how something works to children and then prompting them to conversation about what we have explained. We start with simple things, like turning on and off the light switches in our house. "Look, see how that works? When you flip it up, it turns off. When you flip it down, it turns on. If you go fast, the light flickers on and off." On and on you explain. You talk about electricity. You ask them where they think it comes from. You talk to them about the danger of electricity. Maybe a lineman has to do work on your street. You explain how the man is tending to the electricity. You prompt the child later about the things that were discussed earlier. You give the child new vocabulary and help them with pronunciation. You teach your child about watching your mouth to see how the words are formed. You have the child teach you how to say the made-up words they are making up.

Eventually, and not before too long, your child will develop an imagination. You want to help the child articulate their imagination as fully as possible. At first you will be describing basic attributes of their imaginary friends or the scenes they see in their dreams and daydreams. You will progress from this into *narrative*. The child will explain sequences of events. You play along and include your own imagination. You keep a positive, constructive attitude about the play and you watch it take off. Children develop rich inner lives by having their imaginations cultivated by an engaged parent. Children develop symbology. You have to protect the meaning blocks of their language from being infected by the evils of Woke Disney and other modern, corporate contemporaries. You give life to their language by holding sacred their fascination with the world. They can be drawn into the psychotic, schizophrenic madness of public schooling and mass media, if you are not careful. Children deserve nothing less than excellence. They need the *good stuff* to base their language and symbology off of. They need the classics of antiquity. They need the masculine epics of our Western Canon. They need the brawn of our Post War artists, before America's Cultural Revolution. They need the patriotic and Christian stories that pop up here and there nowadays from an inspired dissident. You cannot inculcate your child with *Stranger Things* and other pro-pedophilia media programming. You must be in charge of how your children acquires language. You have to be nobler than any of your own cynicism or disappointment in the world and allow your child to live in a world of love and sanctity. No child should be exposed to anything other than a loving influence. There is plenty of time in adulthood to be under psychological assault *from without*. Parents should never be complicit in the globalist programming of their children being carried out by billionaires and their ugly, Marxist lackeys.

Instead, children will live in loving lands of their own imagination. They will meet a thousand and one interesting characters who represent the many, wonderful aspects of their personalities. In their imaginations, children will meet angry characters, jealous characters, and a whole host of other types. They will learn to negotiate and then adventure with these characters. The world of their imagination will remind us, at times, of the spiritually mature Middle Ages -when Europeans lived in close communion and intrigue with one another, united under a central morality. There will be bold, noble characters. There will be dainty but cunning princesses. There will be jesters and knaves. There will be monsters and there will be angels. We must foster this imagination in our children so that they are fully self-articulated when they are of the age to participate in the economy. Fables contain timeless lessons and impart values that help us *contribute* when we are older. Our kids do not need *screen time* featuring people of color berating white people for misgendering them. They need to hear about ravens being duplicitous and tricky, foxes being thieves, lions being lazy or brave, dragons devouring everything, and so forth. Traditional stories help our children confront death, fight evil, make a stand for good, and to behave with grace around those less fortunate. The Bible is chock full of these lessons. So are our western fables. We need the Bible and we need the wisdom of antiquity.

Liberals get "triggered" because their parents failed to give them a logically consistent worldview that has explanatory power for all the problems of the world. The more creative liberals were taught to whip up some word storm that delays and disables pertinent moral questions but fundamentally, they all get triggered. Liberals lack meaning. They live in a conceptual world of shortcuts, belligerence, edicts (that were put on them), and catatonia (sometimes expressed as "psychedelia"). They live in a web of intellectual incoherence that refuses to acknowledge itself. Their most fundamental interests were denied in childhood or they twisted and subverted in order to serve a parental agenda. Peaceful parents do better. They know good from evil and they articulate it to their children. They help their children to articulate it, themselves. They develop the stories that are within their children and they use the insights offered from our forefathers to connect the children further to meaning. Liberalism is a relatively new phenomena, with its roots in antiquity coming from open homosexuality precipitating the downfall of civilizations, Satanic death cults, witchcraft, blood sacrifices, orgy cults, genocides, and Middle Eastern paganist cults. Tradition has always been the stabilizing force in the world and its history is much more robust and preserving.

In their imagination, our children will go on a Hero's Journey to make right the wrongs in the world. Wounds will be mended. Debts will be cleared. Evildoers will reform or suffer the natural consequences. Boys will become men. This is the language embedded from birth in the European mind. As peaceful parents, we foster this heroism in our children by continuing with them on the path of articulation. Always we are adding new words, new insights, new meaning, asking our questions to foster their development, and working with them to convey further and further their inner lives. We do not transmit this as some YouTube television program to the world. We hold this process in our private care, not for public spectacle and consumption. To make this public is to deprive our children of the artistic privacy they will need later in life to be moral agents for good. We are set against evil. No need to reveal our children's personal playbooks out of our own need to be seen as a good parent to others. Parents who do this have a problem with vanity and fundamentally have made their children's articulation process *about themselves*, not about their children. The adult world is a world of privacy, not Internet broadcasts of the personal details of children – despite all the YouTubers and Instagrammers making big bucks off of mining their children for pleasure buzz for strangers. Personal disclosure is for personal relationships but people have been dazzled by the Internet and so exploit themselves and their children. The last thing a child needs is the bigotry of Internet comments peppering their inner world or a parent who cannot leave their professional existence to the professional realm.

Children need meaning upon meaning upon meaning!

Individual Attention

We need to set aside time for each child individually, as much as possible. When a parent expects their older children to raise their younger children, the children *all* miss out on crucial, formative experiences with their parents. Chaos forms as children are imperfect parents and resort to the hasty half measures they see their parents use in times of anxiety. Conflicts form and each child develops a yearning for their parent's attention that they cannot articulate on their own. In particular, the boys need time with their father so they have modeled what it means to be a man. The girls need time with their mother for the same reason. Each child needs a special bond with their parents.

When you take the time to get to know each of your children, as everyone ought to, you are better able to address their needs. Plus, you get that special feeling only a parent can have – knowing you are giving your child the blueprints they need to be able to have successful relationships the rest of their life. Devices and social media can only fill deficits for people, such as not having enough fun time in the home or not meeting enough people, but they can never provide what a loving parent who makes lots of eye contact can. Those one-on-one fishing trips, playtimes, short trips to the store, walks around the neighborhood, or whatever else amount to a lot for a child. They also make parenting a less stressful experience. We get so caught up in the broader world, we put ourselves on the hook for so many bills, oftentimes it is nice to commune directly with our children and leave the rest of the world out. They need this every day. We should be giving quality energy to our children as much as our professional lives will allow us. If we have to be weekend warriors, so be it. If we have to back off at work for an hour or two so that when we get home, we will have meaningful energy left in the tank, so be it. We need to give each child the attention they need. It is not always easy but it is the right thing to do – and it pays off big time down the line!

Positive Feedback

As part of peaceful parenting, children need accurate feedback from the learned parent in order to calibrate themselves accurately to their interests and goals. What this means is that children need to know what it is that they do well and how they can improve. Victims of neglect do not get feedback. They get emptiness and pained silence. Victims of verbal abuse get a bunch of crap about how they are not good, how they are failures (which is always parental projection), how they cannot live up to this or that, and how they are "effing it up". Other victims of verbal abuse get parents who dote on the qualities they cannot help about themselves, like being intelligent or beautiful. Peaceful parents can be appreciative of a child's inherent qualities but being recognized for these qualities alone leads to complacency, vanity, and sometimes strange incestual transference from perverted mothers and fathers.

We should be helping our children to take advantage of and develop the aspects of themselves that sustain virtue in the world. With respect to this ethos, let us address inborn features first. If you have a less attractive or less intelligent child, you will need to help the child build a *heart of gold* so that they are compelling to others and happy and confident in themselves. If you have a more attractive or more intelligent child, you will need to help the child build a *heart of gold* so that they are compelling to others and happy and confident in themselves. We know, as a fact, that more attractive and more intelligent people make more money and have preferable life outcomes compared to others. That said, if our kid happened to hit the genetic jackpot, we can only teach them to take advantage of this inborn features – not to deny them and equivocate. Some people are born lucky but with liberal parents, will end up expending their beauty and misusing their intelligence in the service of misleading and hurting others. If a lucky kid is born to peaceful parents, which is hitting the jackpot anyway, beauty and intelligence become assets in the service of virtue in the world – not personal points of vanity. But even well-meaning parents become vain about these qualities, especially when they see their children gain advantages over others. Donald Trump is a great example of hitting the jackpot: an exceptionally intelligent person born to exceptional parents heralding from a long line of excellence. Rather than turning inwardly and becoming a spiteful liberal about it, Donald Trump has flexed his God-given gifts in the service of denying his cowardly haters and building up Middle America. You can win the birth jackpot and turn it into a sweepstakes for good people later on. Melania Trump won the jackpot as well, great looks and high intelligence. She has become the most noble First Lady in American history and a kind of angel for America's Forgotten Children – victims of human trafficking. These people have hearts of gold. They were raised well, far better than the norm for their days. They use their smarts to be effective communicators, champions for free enterprise, and adherents of Jesus Christ.

Our children need their qualities to be tended to and fostered with open feedback. Maybe they are developing into great swimmers. Or they are washing dishes efficiently. Or they are conscientious about some possessions they own. Perhaps they are showing competence in memorizing things, like the story books we are reading them. Or they are physically vigorous and highly athletic. Maybe they are naturally musical. We need to pay close attention to see what natural, often personality based, qualities are coming out in our children and then we need to make these qualities explicitly known to our children. This does not mean we then put expectations on our kids. Kids can develop expectations for themselves by watching us be engaged in our own interests and goal setting around our interests. Children need childhood to be a petri dish of productive experimentation. We offer them this by giving them accurate feedback on what they are good at and by giving them consistent reinforcement through encouragement and curiosity. This will give them the confidence to test themselves against others. Most parents who are ambition conscious will pile expectations onto their child and then *pit* the child against others. Sometimes this works, in that children outperform and rise above, but this is a psychodrama that is fulfilled – not an authentic expression of a championship mindset. True champions are pure of heart and are *closers* because their parents were *closers*. Anyone can win a competition through enough sheer practice and a few natural advantages. Winning on account of a *love for the game*, an existential hero's journey expressed in form through the competition, is the result of *parental love*. Those who are "naturals" were naturally loved by their parents. Achievements are familial and communal in origin, not a narcissistic ambition game carried out by soulless automatons for economic gain and celebrity.

When children can hear, "Hey, you did this well and here's why," or, "You're catching the drift here but focus on this," they have a coherent self-image that they can proceed from or hang up in favor of something else. Our children will eventually know better than us how it is that they will spread virtue in the world but neither should we pretend to be directionless hippies if they have shown a particular proclivity and zest for something they are truly good at. Some people are born statesmen. Some people are born bakers, carpenters, philosophers, cattlemen, scientists, painters, and so forth. Our children often become like us. They inherited most of their personality from us! If I am an author, maybe my child will be an author. That is different from, "My child *should* be an author." Let us not give our kids a case of the shoulds. They get to be what they want to be but beyond that, what they *want* to be may not be what they will be the most fulfilled being. Our job is to make those two consonant, as much as possible. Kids who are peacefully parented have the best shot taking advantage of their natural advantages in an explicit and enjoyable way in order to advance good in the world and bring profits to their loved ones.

Peaceful Parenting As A Community

Parenting is a big, energy consuming job. As we become self-knowledgeable, we recognize more and more the need for people who share our values. We need them around so we can work together toward common goals. A lofty goal to shoot for is to peacefully parent as a community. The focus of this section of the book will be on values transmission. We want others to buy in to peacefully parenting so we do not feel hard pressed to uproot ourselves, travel halfway across the country, and try to settle down near some people we met online that may or may not be good friends but hey, at least they are peacefully parenting. It is far more efficient to convince the people already in your life to buy in on the precepts of peaceful parenting.

You will want to explain, preferably before you have children, to the people in your life why parenting with aggression, manipulation, or neglect is not how you want to do things. If they can abide by the basics, you all will be off to a great start: no spanking, no verbal castigation, no emotional withdrawal, and if the child's behavior is overwhelming, take a deep breath and look for support. These ground rules are sensibly conveyed to others without the need for dipping into politics, talking about the intergenerational transmission of child abuse, or even bringing your conversation "into the personal". These are house rules, like shutting off the lights when you are done using them or not swearing. First World people have a basic empathy and understanding that these are the guidelines that govern their every day, out in the world existence.

The first place to look for community, for most people, is their own parents. Grandparents who are sensible have some idea that they will need to look after the grandchildren in order to earn their keep in old age.

Most often this is disrupted by liberal grandparents, who think they can turn to the state for all their social problems, or by grumpy grandparents that do not want to change with the times. Peaceful parenting is about loving children and its standards challenge even the best of us. Old people need to be willing to be challenged, to a degree, in order to have their place in a young child's life. Children challenge us. Being open to them is a part of helping them learn and grow. Some grandparents simply cannot handle this and so they merit less of a place in a child's life. They may abide by the basics of not engaging in overt abuse but they have little to offer otherwise. They are narcissistic babies and cannot bend the knee for the sake of the next generation. Old people who spent little time as adults in the free market, namely government employees and welfare cases, have significant personal growth impediments that will hamper their ability to be *loving* toward grandchildren. Their version of love will be a manipulation that eases their conscience for the ways in which they failed their own children, if they are even engaged emotionally. The grandchild will be used for emotional comfort, rather than regarded as a burgeoning individual with gifts to nurture. This does not communicate peacefulness and reasoning to a child. It conveys tolerating warm bodies because they share a last name. Children are fully within their bounds to lose their patience with doddering grandparents. This was far less of a problem before the Industrial Revolution because old people *had* to contribute to survive. Now grandparents build up their retirements and do what they please, which is an atomized and narcissistic way to live your life. Happens all the time.

From grandparents we need to expect *respect* for the parents now doing the parenting, the basics of peaceful parenting mentioned earlier, some kind of goodwill effort at engaging with the new ways (which are much like the old ways, minus the Medieval child abuse), and some degree of conceptualization that the torch is being passed. A grandparent may have had a highly successful business and is a supremely capable and lucid individual. That is great news. They will "get with the program" much more quickly than a grandparent who sits around in a recliner, waiting to die. High value grandparents deserve more negotiation and wiggle room when it comes to bringing them into the peaceful parenting fold. They did some things well, or a lot of things well, and they are an easier sell – but it does not mean that they will necessarily be instantly sold on the prospect.

Some grandparents will surprise us. Usually they start with lots of gifts. That is how they know to add value. They do not add value by grace of their personality, which they keep stowed away. We can hold boundaries with people like this. We keep things to shorter visits. We emphasize their presence in the early going, when grandparenting is mostly about holding fussy babies and changing a diaper here and there, in the hopes that they will bond enough to come around to being more reasonable when they are older – and the children are older. Personality is infectious. Children absorb the personalities of those around them, like sponges. Do we want this person around our children? To what degree? Where does their personality shine? How do we keep contact centered around this person's strengths? These can be difficult questions that require rumination. After all, grandparents do not grow on trees. There are only so many elderly people that will be invested in your children, particularly in the shorn social fabric of post mass migration, post television America.

The next place to turn for community is to our friends. The average adult in America is a mess of mild addictions, media inspired sentiments, public school education, and some sense of fun. America is a fun place, in spite of the Left's attempts at making it super duper serious and bitter. Younger adults usually know how to have a bit of fun. We can appeal to them, "Look at the upsides. We parent well. You come around and hang with the kids sometimes. Soon, you'll have kids of your own and you'll join in the fun!" People who do not get going on having children by their early thirties tend to fall out of their friend groups because the friend groups have moved on to parenting. A lot of the point of having friends as an adult is to form bonds that will carry into community. America's underbelly culture, the culture that liberalism spawned, tells us that having friends is about consuming media together, having shallow interactions, shopping together, and trying really hard to have a black friend in the friend group. This is not the true spirit of friendship. Friendship forms loyalty and loyalty helps us to be accountable to one and another in raising the next generation. People who go to church regularly understand this. Our friends inspire us and we keep their company because they are enjoyable to us. Our friends help us to find spouses. Our friends give us something to look forward to. We are in an enterprise together. We have to be united in a common purpose, even if we are only meta and explicit about it once in a blue moon. Friendship needs to be fun. Parenting needs to be fun. Self-seriousness is an outcome of loneliness and isolation, not something we need to test people against. When we parent well, we draw friendly people toward us. You are not supposed to peacefully parent alone on a mountaintop, against all odds. There are good people in the world. You just have to entice them to get involved. You will want to foster the growth of their family. It is in their best interests. That is a team effort.

Extended family is another source of community. So are neighbors. We can also go to church and get to know the congregation there. Or we grew up in a church congregation and people are on board with peaceful parenting. We also can find consonance with our coworkers, especially outside of corporate or governmental settings. We have different boundaries for the different levels of relationships. Some people will be very close to us and we will expect more of them. Some people will be more distant and we will be happy with just an occasional visit, here and there. What matters is that we get off our butts and find as much like-mindedness as possible for this great peaceful parenting undertaking.

Chapter Six: Practical Applications

This is not a homeschooling guide but I would be remiss in leaving out a section on practical applications. We have covered how negotiation works in the early going parenting. Now we can cover some of the basic lessons we can teach to our children through peaceful parenting that will prepare them to generate virtue in the world autonomously. We will cover moral challenges, critical aspects of self-knowledge, and topics that will prepare our children to have successful relationships. We have covered some of these from an adult angle, earlier in the book, but this section is specifically geared toward instructing children. Some topics have been covered sufficiently already, such as the question of using or not using sugar in parenting.

Lying

It will dawn on a child that people do not tell the truth. Sadly, for most kids this comes from their first heartbreak, when a parent betrays their trust. For a peacefully parented child, this realization will come when the child is near or of the age of reason and in contact with the broader world. We prepare the child for this day by telling them about lying: how it works and why people do it.

Lying is performative because the world is in competition or it is because people are evil. Good people are forced to lie, by evil people, in order to protect themselves. Lying in self-defense is not immoral. The more government power concentrated in a society, the more people have to lie to some degree in order to make a living for themselves – whether it is by advancing the interests of the evil system or by maintaining appearances in order to get some money and keep one's sanity. If there is a powerful man who extracts money from every single person in your area, who uses it inefficiently and immorally, and fully expects to extract money from you when you have some money, will you tell him the truth – that you do not want to pay him money – or will you pay him the bribe and try to get on with your life? This is the situation of the modern West. Troubled, wealthy, liberal men who came before us decided to steal from future generations in order to give "healthcare" (a 1960's liberal invention) and retirement security to existing generations. Men who came before us decided to institute a central currency and bank that they could manipulate and control in order to enrich themselves at the expense of everyone else. The entire social and economic existence of the modern West is built upon the lies of these men and the apathy of their contemporaries. What is worse is that there are lots and lots of people, educated by public schools, who think this world order is the *just* and *sane* world order and that there has never existed anything else. These people form a titanic voting block that votes to make life harder for everyone else by increasing the power of those few elite who established this world order. Speaking out against this giant voting block gets you "cancelled" – you lose significant opportunities to participate in the dollar economy.

Children need to understand that peacefulness is not the way of the world, especially the Third World. Peacefulness exists to whatever degree a person can freely associate in their personal and professional lives. The elite want everyone mixed up and interacting against their wills because when smart, First World people are separate and distinct, they start to eject the weird, global elite that have come into their midst. The parasitism of the global elite withers and dies. The elite hate this and they try to kill anyone who seeks to sever this unfair relationship. It is like having a neighbor who thinks he gets to pet your dogs whenever he wants, take milk from your fridge whenever, kiss your mom sometimes, and take your toys if he pleases. He is annoying, evil, and a serious pain in the ass but he has convinced enough people to let him do it that he has become rich and so he can put *your* money into the pockets of a thousand and one people who will speak highly of him. This is also known as the media. The media lies about the nature of this perverted evildoer and since everyone gets their information from the media, and their high dollar production value lends them credibility (they look more professional and credible), everyone is trained to believe that standing against the lies is what racists, white nationalists, terrorists, incels, and dictators do.

We can go even more basic on lies and suppose to our children, out loud, that we are going to lie about something. We have taught them that the color red is red but now we are pretending it is not red. It is blue, instead. So, we point to red and say "blue". Then we tell them that they can only have their glass of raw milk with dinner if they guess the color correctly. They say "red", as is natural to them, and we exclaim that actually the correct answer was blue. This will provoke a lot of anger and confusion in them, if we conduct this experiment too early. They have to have signaled to us their interest in what lying is, before we set out to do this. When the experiment comes to pass, we need to ask our children what they think about their internal states of anger and confusion. How does it feel to be lied to and then tricked? Is this something we naturally do without all these caveats, explanations? Do we do this to one another as part of our standards around the house? These feelings, are they inspirational and fun or are they taxing and burdensome? Do we seek to provoke this sense of wrongdoing in one another or are we negotiating and reasoning our way through these feelings when they inadvertently

155

come up? *NOW*, do people out in the world care as much about honesty as we do? Which ones do and which ones do not? Who is particularly uninterested in what their lies do to us? How do we spot these people? What do they look like?

At this juncture, we also have to teach our children about reciprocity, which should be its own category in this chapter. There people who will want to win favor with us by being honest and sharing the same interests and values. There are people who will want to favor with us by lying to us and "favor" to them means that we will be silent or complicit in their thievery and debauchery. When people meet us in reality, that is to say that they are sober and in their right mind and honest, we benefit from meeting *them* in reality. When both parties are aligned with truth, people just get along. The catch is that there are a *lot* of dishonest people out there. In fact, most people on the planet do not have good politics. Their politics are dysfunctional and this is an intellectual outcropping of their personalities. Civilization is exceptional. The norm has been barbarity and continues to be, in most of the world. We are going to go out into this world and will have to find our way. We will need an internal moral compass to tell us what is right and wrong. How our parents treated us and whether they were curious or not about our internal states will make up the substance of that compass. If we were peacefully parented, we will meet people everywhere we go who do not have the same quality of internal compass. They are going to want or expect things of us that are not accurate to who we are or consonant with the value we have to give. When they run into this disconnect, instead of self-reflecting, they are going to attack us or lose interest in us. The world is filled with people we can collaborate with and love but also filled with people who will lack our goodness. We have to learn to have *fair exchanges* with people of all different stripes. We cannot just go around performing citizen's arrests on everyone or being eternally frustrated at everyone's inefficiency. We need a way of leveraging ourselves upwards in a society full of people who were not peacefully parented. We find this way by looking for *reciprocity.*

Reciprocity is the principle of mutual exchange and the bedrock of what used to be called "capitalism", until liberals hijacked the term and turned everyone's opinion against it in the last two generations until it effectively became a toxic brand to be avoided. Without engaging in a noble crusade to revive the term, we can still examine what reciprocity is. Reciprocity is value for value *without manipulation.* People exchange their labor for wages. Employers give employees money and in exchange, the employees bring in profit for the business. Our lawn needs mowing, we are willing to give our kid a few bucks to mow it. Sometimes people forgo being paid here and now in the promise that they will get something better down the line. That is what parenting is. Parents have children and raise them well so that one day, the children will help them out and enrich their lives in a myriad of ways, and because raising children enlivens parents with joy, satisfaction, intrigue, and love. Value for value, with exceptional children, can mean a parent is employed by their child in some business relatively early in the child's adulthood. Such cases do happen! Or value for value means telling a kid, "I will give you a piece of fruit if you eat the beef on your plate." The kid gets the fruit, the parent gets the satisfaction of knowing the child has more animal protein in their systems.

Apart from money, reciprocity has important personal and professional considerations for our children. Our kids have personal and professional needs they will try to full when they interact with this challenging world. When they choose their friends, our children need to know *why* a certain person is a good friend. Do these kids derive mutual enjoyment and learning from their friendship or it is a drag for one or both of them? When our kids are deciding what they want to do for a living, will they be able to derive enough professional satisfaction from their vocation to be able to stick with it or to feel motivated to leverage it into something else down the line? Will the vocation or profession "reciprocate" sufficiently for them? Or with fitness, will we be able to make the value proposition to them that remaining fit throughout their teenage and adult years will yield to them the value that will motivate them to consistently work out and keep in shape?

Addictions shortcut the natural reciprocity process. Addictions give us temporary pleasure that *feels* like value and that we may even build other things on top of but ultimately hamper our ability to make long term reciprocity assessments. Eating a bag of greasy chips is a tastier, easier proposition than eating a bag of vegetable greens, but it leaves us overweight and demotivated. Stealing money from a cash register lets us spend now but we lose reputation and maybe even go to jail, which is a permanent mark on us. People who are addicts to the financial political system outlined just a few paragraphs ago will find plenty of reinforcement from the carnal world to continue on as if there is nothing wrong with them. These people lose their ability to know genuine value from *fiat*, which is an illusion of value. A cavalcade of fake friends may win you homecoming queen but will those people support you for long or truly care about you when you get pregnant the night of homecoming? People build up fiat in their personal, emotional lives. When those bubbles pop, people have crises. They can either become self-knowledgeable and look for *true value* or they can declare bankruptcy and slowly nurse back to "health" all their unhealthy habits. Parenting with rewards and punishments is the basis by which fiat is formed in the world. Whether rewards and punishments yield desired outcomes, after the fact, is simply a matter of behavior programming and whether the resource environment will support the behavior programming. We decide to punish or reward because it is more convenient than reasoning and negotiating. Convenience becomes the prevailing standard. Fiat forms and then addictions are built on top of that fiat. America can house 2,000,000 prisoners because future generations are stolen from in order to conveniently "put people away" for their crimes, instead of forcing them to give accurate restitution to their victims. The bankers who run America use the candy of currency inflation and the punishment of jail cell "time outs" in their parenting. In doing so, they short circuit people's natural gauge for reciprocity and simply offer themselves up as the cure to the problem they are inducing in the people beneath them. Same goes for parents who abuse their children and use rewards and punishments instead of peaceful parenting.

When our children are looking for reciprocity out in the world, they have to know if they are bringing value to the table or not. We would be awful narcissists to say to them, "Well, I have peacefully parented you, which is a value that most people were not raised with, therefore just get out there and you will provide value!" This is something akin to the 1980's Self-Esteem movement, which told people that because they *existed*, they were worthy. This has led to a lot of bitterly disappointed adults in the economy who never rose above middle management. Being peacefully parented is a wonderful foundation but our children need skills and economic value in order to compete in a society that will not readily just flop over in adoration and enchantment because our kid was raised well. Most people out in the world simply will not have the sensitivity, awareness, or cognitive tools to recognize what is great about our kids. The mass of lower IQ and lower empathy people in the world are generally conspiring to destroy intelligent, high empathy people. We need to empower our children, beyond the peaceful parenting, with First World technical, communication, business enterprise, time management, and negotiation skills so that they can raise many of their own children, far above the fray of nihilistic socialism that has blanketed the globe. A peacefully parented child, with no technical skills, will likely stay out of poverty. A peacefully parented child raised with technical excellence, whether in oratory, management, finance, engineering, entrepreneurship, or some other discipline in the same bailiwick, will be upwardly mobile.

Sure, there will be a few peacefully parented people who land on working a production line or will be wage employees in a store for the majority of their adult years but peaceful parenting removes so many of the *preventable* personal impediments that keep people stuck in these professional roles. Peacefully parented kids perceive higher and higher value propositions and reciprocity agreements, as they mature and come into their full mental faculties. Their perception improves, thanks to our helping them so much to have clarity of thinking, and they take leadership positions in the economy. Asian parenting values technical prowess but uses rewards and punishments. Because of their higher relative IQs, Asians in the West have great earning power but tend to vote toward totalitarianism and are not often in executive leadership. Western parenting, currently, places a high value on self-worth and a lower value on technical mastery. When Westerners work in the East Asian economy, they often find themselves in leadership or subleadership positions of influence but are not as often brought in for their staying power as technical workers. Westerners train East Asians to do the technical work, which is not the same as being a large part of the technical workforce itself.

Anger

For young children, anger most commonly comes from something not going the child's way. The child wants to linger inside a store, or go visit a neighbor's pet when it is freezing outside, or to stay in the bathtub for a long, long time. Spikes in anger for the child are natural. We have to patiently attend to their anger and explain to them where the gap is between what they want to happen and what we need to happen in order to keep a rhythm in the home. Children thrive off of patterns, structure, and consistency – even if they fight against these things almost every step. The authority of the parent involves administrating the structure of the homelife. Keeping a structure in the home becomes ever more important as the couple births more children and incorporates their wants and needs into the overall picture.

Children get angry because they do not understand how things around the home work. They want a baby gate to close when it is already closed. They want a window open when it scorching outside. They throw things down the steps and then trip on those things later. All sorts of chaos is unleashed onto the home when kids are learning and experimenting. Being a parent means constantly negotiating between the child's slowly resolving chaos, the family's structure and home life rhythm, and the needs of the parents. Sometimes parents bite off more than they can chew, like the father wanting to keep a leather chair in the living room when a toddler is learning to write with markers. A mother may want to keep a china hutch in a nook and find the display glass is broken from an errant whack of a toy broom. Parents are responsible for every single thing that happens in the home. The kid touches a hot stove and then screams for a half hour in terrible fury and sorrow? That is the parents' fault and responsibility. Parents compound the anger of their children when they are not orderly themselves. Parental chaos annoys and frustrates children. To help facilitate children learning to understand how things work in the home, parents either need to keep the home tidy and clean or they need to become committed minimalists – which is usually a weird, liberal renouncement of responsibility.

Another reason why children get angry is because one or both parents are *weak*. Peaceful parenting does not mean being a soft, semi-effeminate libertarian who clutches to their child because of a lack of meaningful and challenging adult relationships. To ensure quality of parenting, parents have to be assertive with their leadership in the home. Negotiating with your child does not mean that you plead, or you explain things ad nauseum to no discernible effect, or you become so autistically devoted to gentleness that your kid eventually figures out they can just walk over you when you are in the way, or treat you with annoyance because you are a "nice guy". Children with weak parents end up resenting their parents, feeling near constant annoyance with their parents, and will respond with anger to disagreements. This is because when a parent is weak, the parent is putting the parenting burden onto the child. By being weak, the parent cedes more responsibility (or is outright neglectful) to the child than the child is prepared for. This crosses the child's boundaries. Children are not born perfectly civilized little aristocrats. They can be rough and tumble. They can be animalistic. They can be wild and tough. A parent needs to "roll with it" on these rougher aspects of a child so that they child feels mirrored, empathized with, and can tether themselves to an understanding parent figure that will guide them to solid ground. This does not mean fighting with your child. It means allowing your child to see how you resolve things with your own, rational anger. Your child may break something expensive of yours. You feel anger come up. Do you wear it on your face or swallow it down? You wear it on your face only to the degree that is it a healthy expression *and* you do not overwhelm your child. Parental anger becomes a teaching tool in this sense but weak parents are not in touch with their healthy anger. In peaceful parenting circles, this most often happens with parents so devoted to conceptual ideals that they forget to act like human beings.

The last way we will discuss anger coming up for our children is around boundaries. Anger lets us know when someone is disrespecting us. The world is filled with insolent, falsely certain, midwit, traumatized, and socialist boundary crossers. Our children will have to learn to navigate social circumstances. There will be children they encounter at the park or on the playground who are little turds, reflections of their parents, of course. These children will piss off our kids. They may shove our kid to get on the slide first, scream like savages in our kid's face, or name-call our kid. This is not an opportunity for our kid to beat the hell out of another kid. Lots of parents think it is and they live their unlived revenge fantasies through their kids, signing them up for unending, boring karate classes. Rather, this is an opportunity for our kid to feel their anger, see if the situation is salvageable, scan their parental options, and then decide what they want to do. Libertarian parents teach a mantra of "principled disengagement". Just give up the slide to the bully. Just shrug your shoulders and feel narcissistically special that you do not need to resort to violence like all these other brutes (which is a parental bigotry). Peaceful parents do no err in this way, despite what some other peaceful parenting "experts" out there are peddling. Rather, a peaceful parent helps hone their children's anger by teaching them to feel it, to consult it among other feelings when considering a course of action, and to stand up for oneself when someone is placing themselves firmly into the child's plans. Who gets to go down the slide *means something*, despite what namby pamby, Montessori libertarians with parenting blogs and video channels "teach" us. Principled disengagement with a good dose of "compassion" after the fact is just cowardice masquerading as nobility. This is the mantra of *losers*. Sometimes life is rough. Bad people, or good people in a bad mood, get in the way. We do not have to fight every idiot who slights us but the slide at the playground is emblematic of the institutions in the Commons. Either you use it, as is your patrimony, or some dingleberry numbskull will bump you out of the way and keep it all to herself. The West's institutions *mean something*, they are not just statist or "religulous" false gods to be deconstructed like a smarmy know-it-all. We need *winners* to rise up again. We need parents to raise their kids to lead society by conquering evil. The emphasis on self-knowledge in this book means first we conquer evil in ourselves but then we go out in the world and *make deals*. Getting tough with bullies means making deals with them, turning them, ordering them around, and civilizing them. Sometimes it means getting gruff or stern with them and when they leave us no option, which is highly unlikely to happen in childhood nowadays but *did* happen when children were allowed to roam around a lot more

(in major American cities before public schooling fully took off),
sometimes we have to physically contain a bully.

Before pedophile Satanists and vaccine clutching globalists
dumped the Third World into the First, we as children were out in the
world. We were engaged. There were highly sophisticated social networks
of children learning to be adults. Kids ran around in the suburbs and
before forced integration, in the cities. Things got rough and tumble. As a
peaceful parent, you are going to want to wrestle with your sons. This is
not child abuse. They may take an interest in a punching bag you keep in
the garage. This is not automatically because you yourself were raised
with corporal punishment and have not processed it fully. Our verbal
jousting finds its way into physical expression, usually with us walking
softly but carrying a big stick. People who get some dose of contact sports
in childhood have a toughness about them that serves them well later on.
Again, this is not a call to you to teach your kid to fight the world or fight
every fight that comes his or her way. It means that sometimes the land is
not peaceful and is in dire need of peacemakers. Peace is forged. It does
not come as a result of everyone reading this book on peaceful parenting
simultaneously, collapsing and writhing on the ground, and then standing
up and we suddenly live in an anarcho-capitalist Montessori paradise
where nobody pays taxes and we all have quadruple our current net
worth.

Children need to know what their anger is good for. It is good
for a lot!

Pornography and Adultery

There are "attractions" out in the world that will hijack our attention. We
are hardwired to want sugar, fat, salt, and sex, among other things. Some
crazy liberal parents will expose their children to pornography and then
attempt to talk the child through what pornography is. You do not have

to expose your kid to toxic attractions in order for them to be inoculated against them. As they enter into puberty, you are going to need to explain how pornography is rampant throughout the world, how it is a revolutionary weapon run by hostile outsiders to wreck Western Civilization, how Westerners have always had strong objections to indecency, and how it latches onto people's unmet romantic love needs and erodes people until they become insatiable, complacent love cripples. You will want to guide them to healthy expressions of courtship, kinship, and interest in the opposite sex. They need your encouragement to help them understand how flirting and bonding with a member of the opposite sex builds trust and improves one's overall life prospects. In a locked down world, this is a difficult prospect, but this is where you have to leverage your personal networks. If you do not have personal networks to leverage or there are few kids your child's age in your networks, you are going to have to go above and beyond so that your kid does not find themselves stranded in the purgatory of trying to build in-person relationships through social media.

There is a strong element of *seeking* when it comes to dating. You are not helping your kids by being a couch potato. You need friends and acquaintances who have children. You need to succeed at your job so that there are people around. You need to save your money so that if when your kid becomes a teenager and they want to attend some private school or academy where they can make more friends, you will be able to cover the tuition fees.

Porn is only addictive in relation to the absence of rewarding in-person friendships a person has.

We want to teach our children the value of commitment to our spouse by remaining faithful, renewing and building the marriage as we age, and pointing out what happens to people who cheat. Adultery is wrong and it hurts trust. People who cheat have needs they feel they cannot fill in the relationship and so they look elsewhere. Self-knowledge far in advance staves off these problems. People need to pair up early their adulthoods and get to having children while their bodies are still young. Conscientious men and women should never settle in who they select. They should aim high and land among the stars. People need to act assertively and in a timely manner with matters of the heart, or drift will set in. People who had cheater parents need to come to terms with the destruction their imperfect parents wrought and resolve themselves not to commit the same mistakes. People need to stay away from pornography because it distorts expectations. Adultery is the spawn of insecurities. The insecurity can be a personal neuroticism *or* it can be a real lack in the social environment itself that went unaddressed because the person was less self-knowledgeable or aware earlier in life. Many men and women wake up to their real worth later in adulthood and find themselves in intolerable arrangements with spouses who are stuck and do not want to grow. Usually, though, people cheat because they have pornbrain, as discussed earlier in this book, or because feminism turned them into greedy whores with careers. We are rewarded the earlier we do the work of self-discovery. Most parents in America just sit back and watch their grown children amble idly into the dating pool. We have to do better. Our kids should know what they want and how they will get it before they have left the nest around age eighteen.

Device Addiction

Devices are engineering to be addicting. People's screen time average increases every year and people over the age of eighteen now average a whopping 13 hours a day on devices.[60] People cede their children over to media since they find parenting to be emotionally exhausting and they have shallow inner lives that can be imparted to their children fully with

---

[60] https://eyesafe.com/covid-19-screen-time-spike-to-over-13-hours-per-day/

just a few sentences once in a while. The more conscientious parents that exist out there right now give their kids access to smartphones and TVs before their kids' brains are ready and hope that discussions about the addictive nature of devices will suffice. This is almost correct. Children should not have access to devices until they are teenagers and are finding their economic function in the world. Children under the age of 12 or 13 should not have access to devices. Parents have to lead here by not being addicted to devices themselves.

Humans socialized just fine before the Internet. Devices improve economic productivity, in *some cases*, and allow us to combat globalism, in *some cases*. Devices are a double-edged sword. You would not be reading this book if it were not for your device and for a certain content publisher that has ridden the Internet wave to mega-wealth. At the same time, we do see quite clearly that some people, women in particular, are perpetually overwhelmed by media input and their thinking is hampered, not helped. Some people do not want to have inner lives and simply live through their smartphones and push their true feelings under. We have to tend to the seeds of an inner life in our children so much so that when the *wave* of devices, media exposure, and Internet hits them in adulthood, they will have an internal compass and will be able to maintain a healthy relationship to these things for themselves. Being overwhelmed by media freezes people's maturity and personality development in time. We want our children to continue to grow all through their adulthoods and to reach wisdom in old age. Therefore, premature device exposure is a mistake that grants children more agency than they actually possess.

How To Navigate Authority

There is authority from wisdom and competence and there is authority from power. We want our children to learn to trust our authority by being competent and self-knowledgeable parents. When we practice our power over them, that is to dominate, cajole, threaten, or withdraw –

children become habituated to authorities that are tyrannical, unreasonable, fickle, and punitive. Bad parenting prepares children to become totalitarians as adults. Good parenting habituates children to become defenders of freedom and order as adults.

We teach children to handle authority by asking them about who they think does something well. Why does that person do what they do so well? What steps did they have to take? Does being good at that make them a good parent, a good person, a good leader, or simply good at the thing they do? For example, is a talented drug dealer better or worse prepared to lead society compared to a guy who runs a successful plumbing company? They are both competent. One, however, is wise. The other is cunning. Wisdom comes from moral exchange. Cunning comes from criminal enterprise.

In our own lives, we work with authority by finding good people or good ideas that we serve, usually economically, as experts, technicians, salesmen, advocates, or servants. We gain authority and with that authority comes responsibility over the lives of others. Authority, however small, teaches each one of us how to better take care of our fellow man by creating value. This value is not always measured economically, because so much of today's society is based in fiat, but more often than not - it is.

People with authority have a larger say than people with less authority. This is hard to understand for some people, who were raised to think "one person one vote" is the right way to run society. People with more authority generally have a lot more invested than the common person in whether an idea or an enterprise succeeds or fails. That is because they have put so much responsibility in. We look to these people for leadership but we also allow for outside ideas, upstarts, outliers, and natural talent for authority, as well. In the United States, in particular, we have a tradition of honoring people who are "too good to ignore". This has been perverted by the media through its promotion of false endeavors wherein people who are skilled at inconsequential endeavors are lionized and artificially propped up. This is not to say that something like professional basketball can be fully reduced to "who puts a ball through a hoop the best", as athletic prowess does have some marketable entertainment value, but it does mean that athletes are not authorities in politics, supply chain management, philosophy, food production, etc. The media bestows prestige, through corporate advertising, foreign government money laundering, and regional government subsidies, upon people who are simply good at athletics and winning athletic competitions. This does not grant these people moral authority unless they take the principles of winning athletic competitions and apply them on themselves through self-knowledge in order to become honest, morally excellent people.

Property ownership is something that increases people's authority. Owning habitable land, one step further. Owning tillable land, even one step further. This is because property ownership is a condition that requires maintenance and increases a person's responsibilities. If a person loses ownership, they lose some authority. Before the globalist political revolution, where a managerial super state has been brought into being to be administrated by credentialed liberals, the main people who had authority in society were land and production owners. As the government has gobbled up more and more property and industries into its belly, the people who more and more have authority and call the shots are bureaucrats and the super wealthy. This is most easily explained to our children by explaining to them how a teacher in a public school has more and more false authority every year over our children, compared to us. This is a strange and nonsensical arrangement, is it not? The teacher might even be a good parent themselves, have all the necessary credentials, and generally be a good person (though it is harder and harder to find good people in public service these days) and still it would be a strange arrangement because the teacher is an authority *outside* of our family. Instead of a hostile or foreign elite, the people who run our society should be related to us as closely as possible. Our Western institutions should be run by Western people. Outsiders are not authorities but can sometimes offer good advice, though usually not.

We give our children authority when we place possessions in their care and teach them the skills they need to be their best in the marketplace. We will not be the greatest astronaut or firefighter they will ever know but we should strive to be the absolute best parent they could possibly have. From this love bond comes the certainty they will need to judge good authority from wicked cunning when they are adults. We should be entrusting to our children a larger and larger share of our family enterprise as they age, especially as they become authoritative.

Becoming A Parent

Our children are going to become parents one day themselves. We can ask them what they have appreciated about our parenting thus far, what they would like improved, and what they have not enjoyed. This critical feedback process, where our children are enjoined to offer their opinion directly on our parenting, helps them to conceive of their future role as a parent themselves. Empathy flows both ways as they get to put themselves in *our* shoes and begin to understanding what it must be like to be a parent. Some parents do this abusively with the age-old line, "See how *hard* it is to be your parent?" They do this in a shaming manner. We are doing it in a much different spirit. We are inviting feedback on our parenting as if it were an art, a discipline separate from ourselves. We are driving a car called Parenting and sometimes we miss a turn, sometimes we shift too early or too soon, and sometimes the seats need a cleaning. Though we have a gigantic personal stake in our parenting outcomes, we need to separate ourselves from the process conceptually so that we can retain our objectivity. We are raising our children to think more clearly than we were able to, when we were their age. This means that they will be able to conceive of things amiss or awry that we may not be able to. Add on top of that that at least the father in every peacefully parented household will have a breadwinning job to add to the mix.

Kids get to have a say, always. We take their say into our council and look for objective improvements. The arts are objective, not subjective. In dance, there are certain movements that are more correct than others. Same goes for communication or driving or whatever else. We are humble servants of the truth, not all-knowing demi-gods. Our children are going to parent one day. They need to know the nuts and bolts of what is going on. They need to be able to piece things apart, without our interference, in order to understand how parenting works. We have to stand back sometimes and let them experiment, test us, and even fail, when their failure does not put them in danger. Parenting is more of a, "Look what I have built, son. See how it works?" situation more than it is a, "I never made a mistake ever and you are *just a child*, so back off!" kind of situation. Only people who are ashamed of the job they did are unwilling to allow their children to scrutinize their parenting. Instead, we need to ask, "How has my parenting been for you?" and we need to use our empathy skills to best judge the answer to this question. Our children will tell us. Our hearts will tell us. We want our children to choose us, if they had the choice.

Our children keep us honest to peaceful parenting with their natural responses to things. They cry when under duress. They explain, out loud, an intensely emotional situation between husband and wife. They track sequences of events with remarkable clarity. We want to remain humble and take this crucial data into account when we explain to them how parenting works. We know, in our hearts, when we have failed to live up to our standards. We can either pass this self-deception on to our kids by tricking them into idealizing our parenting, or we can do the right thing and admit fault and work to restore trust. When you are a committed peaceful parent, empowered by the contents of this book, you are likely not to run into catastrophic breaches of trust. Most, if not all, problems will be hiccups along the way. Your children will get to see your humanity. You are a person in progress and your faults do not shake the boundaries of the parent-child relationship. Parents need to be careful with this attitude, however, as it can be used to excuse their misbehaviors. Alcoholics take this attitude and nobly tell themselves that their children will not end up like them because their children see their faults. There is a difference between an acknowledgement of fault with complacent acceptance and an acknowledgement of fault with an obvious, sincere and continuing commitment to improvement.

Logistically, teenagers will need to be taught the rigors and responsibilities associated with parenting. A teenage sibling can be put in charge of a younger sibling, in order to demonstrate this. Or teenagers can work in a daycare or as a teacher's assistant or tutor. We teach our teens the relevant facts about pair bonding, money mastery, and the joys of becoming a parent early in adulthood. We go over the large section in this book about what peacefully parenting *is not*. We encourage our kids to grow up, get real, and start their own families. We play matchmaker by leveraging our networks and we empower our kids by giving them control of some of our investments. The next generation comes into being and we settle into our caretaking roles as attendant grandparents. When our kids are teens and as they show themselves capable, which they always do (when peacefully parented!), we ease back from our role as alpha in the family and grant them their times to shine. Peaceful parenting is a multi-generational enterprise.

Words of Reassurance

Peaceful parenting will challenge even the best of us, the challenge is baked in. We are raising our children better than we were raised. Our children will have more awareness, more agency, and more willpower than we were once allowed to have. Beyond that, we start to experience cognitive decline around age 30.[61] Our memory declines and our IQ slowly drops. Our bodies, especially women's bodies, are aged by parenting. We experience a loss of physical vitality just as our kids are bursting with energy and physical vigor. This is a taxing process! But it is made worth it by building a quality bond with our children. There are going to be times where we lose our patience, get frustrated with losing stuff around the house, get sticker shock at unexpected bills in the mail, or feel tempted to simply grin and bear it, instead of taking care of ourselves like we need to. Hopefully this book makes your parenting process more efficient and leaves with a conception of new options for difficulties that you were formerly just barreling through as best you knew how. We all can use a pick-me-up as parents. Peaceful parenting in a community goes a long way in helping us. So can some sympathy. Parenting is the most rewarding job there is and sometimes, it really is a job. There are long hours: nights of little sleep followed by taxing days of meeting the needs of our little ones. Our commitment to reasoning and negotiating makes a night and day different *and* it is the most efficient way of parenting possible, since there are no damaging aftereffects to then tend to. Weary or tired parents can take heart in knowing that there will always be a corner turned and it all pays off in the end.

---

[61] https://www.sciencedaily.com/releases/2013/08/130807155352.htm

Afterword

This book is a start. There are so many more topics to cover. We will save them for another day. My hope is that by reading this book, you feel much more prepared to start your family or to continue your parenting with some improvements here and there.

Parents who raise their children peacefully can count on a wonderful love bond being formed. In this manner, children and parents form a bond much closer than "best friendship". Our capacity for intimacy is unending, if we just commit to reasoning for our guidance. Some of psychology attempts to mimic a philosophical relationship by offering mantras like, "Always listen to that voice inside of you" or "Return to curiosity, again and again". These are truisms but they are not necessarily accurate to every situation we find ourselves in. Sometimes, the voice inside of us runs into better reasoning that we then have to incorporate. A child will make observations and form arguments that we cannot. After all, we are peacefully parenting so they will one day stand on our shoulders. Or with curiosity, sometimes our kids will lose control because they do not yet have the words to articulate themselves. They will feel angry at us for offering doe-eyed curiosity instead of what they need, which is containment and restraint. The story of Jesus and his disciples caught in a squall on a boat comes to mind. He tempers the storm by saying, "Peace, be still." Our children need to be rooted in our certainty but we only find this certainty through living a truly moral and decent life. We cannot fake our way through peaceful parenting. We have to know ourselves deeply so that we can know our children deeply. We have to be the respite from the world for our children. Our mothers will be the cozy hearth and our fathers the shining castle on the hill. Our children will live in waking delight and together we will celebrate in the sweetness of life. It is this love bond that makes it all worth it. The long conversations amounted to glory. The moments of personal temperance kept us out of the trouble that plagued our forefathers. The team effort of bringing others under the banner gave us and our children *options* going forward.

We do well to honor that love bond as we go along. We are kindling a great fire that will sweep across the civilized world. The change starts in our home. We need to look upon our children with adoration and fascination, again and again. We make that magical eye contact that only parents and their children can make. We hold our children's innocence in our care. We make the home into a place of enchantment. We bring our children into the world as fully functioning beings, free of trouble and ready to lead the way.

Enjoy the book?

Leave it a review on Amazon and Goodreads to help the author build an audience.

Made in United States
North Haven, CT
10 February 2023